ZERO HOUR

100 YEARS ON: VIEWS FROM THE PARAPET OF THE SOMME

The original, hand-annotated panoramas contained in this book are being
exhibited at the Sladmore Contemporary gallery over the centenary of the
battle. For enquiries, please contact:

Sladmore Contemporary
32 Bruton Place, London W1J 6NW

Tel +44 (0)20 7499 0365
Email info@sladmore.com

Poster prints of the panoramas can be ordered through the author's website:
www.jolyonfenwick.com

ZERO HOUR

100 YEARS ON: VIEWS FROM THE PARAPET OF THE SOMME

JOLYON FENWICK

P

PROFILE BOOKS

For R.A.F.F.

First published in Great Britain in 2016 by
Profile Books Ltd
3 Holford Yard
Bevin Way
London WC1X 9HD
www.profilebooks.com

10 9 8 7 6 5 4 3 2 1

Copyright © Jolyon Fenwick 2016

The moral right of the author has been asserted.

A CIP catalogue record for this book is available from the British Library.

ISBN: 978 1 78125 708 1

Project editor: Paul Forty at Brookes Forty *www.brookesforty.com*
Maps by Martin Lubikowski at ML Design *www.facebook.com/makingmapswork*
Text design: Matt Wilson
Typeset in Adobe Jenson Pro

Printed and bound in Italy by L.E.G.O. SpA

The front and back endpapers show overlapping sections of a top-secret hand-drawn British trench map of 1916 (57D S.E.4 Edition 2.B OVILLERS) used by commanders in planning the 1 July attack. The original of the map is in the collection of the Imperial War Museum Department of Printed Books.

CONTENTS

Introduction 6

INTRODUCTION

We remember the Great War of 1914–18 for the numbers of dead and the grief of a generation. But it is not the scale of the suffering alone that makes our remembering seem inevitable. There also appears to be a deliberate artfulness to its narrative; it contains so many of the ironies that make tragic stories stick.

After all, no storyteller could do better than begin their tale at the end of the most glorious summer in living memory, with vast, cheering crowds waving flags at the declaration of war; or than spread the belief that the war would be over by Christmas, and have schoolboy soldiers fibbing about their age so they wouldn't miss it, then shooting their feet off to come home. One could hardly improve on having generals in jodhpurs, and regiments riding off to war, or dividing the classes like different species, then making them share a hole in the ground; or setting the action just a boat ride across the Channel, so that officers could eat breakfast in their dugout and dinner in their club, and London theatre-goers could hear the sound of the guns. A dramatist could only dream of setting great European empires at odds and then bringing them to their knees, or making the enemy of a nation the cousin of its king; or casting both sides as fellow Christians, each sure that Christ would side with them; or

endowing a generation with a culture of grace and tenderness and then blowing them all to bits.

Almost all the great British enterprises on the Western Front took a share in this tragically ironic whole. But one battle brought with it additional ironies of its own. It was fought around a number of small villages on the gently rolling French countryside of Picardy in the summer and autumn of 1916, but it took its name from the river Somme to the south of the battlefield.

The Battle of the Somme was the great offensive that the British people had demanded. The final months of 1914 had been difficult, and 1915 had been worse. But the old certainty persisted that Britannia didn't lose. Civilians and government had allowed the British generals their failed experiments of the previous year, but this time General Sir Douglas Haig, commander of the British Army in France, would put Teutonic barbarism to the sword once and for all. And the normal service of global British benevolent dictatorship would resume.

The belief in certain victory was also underpinned by the introduction of a new kind of army. An army who were all friends. These were men from the same villages, towns, factories, cricket teams and public schools, who had waited patiently outside their local recruiting offices to enlist in August 1914. The British people believed that these civilian 'pals' units would naturally outclass the servile martial professionalism of the enemy. And right up until the final seconds, the volunteer soldiers believed it too.

The battle plan was familiar in format, but novel in scale. The British would attack with thirteen divisions along a fifteen-mile front (after subjecting the Germans to a bombardment of over 1.5 million shells) and force a break in the enemy line that the cavalry would then exploit. The objective was the town of Bapaume, ten miles up the old Roman road from the British lines. It was expected to be taken within three days.

West of Amiens, General Sir Hubert Gough's cavalry waited, all 30,000 of them – Dragoon Guards, hussars, lancers, Life Guards, Royal Horse Guards and the turbaned ranks of the Poona, Hodson's and Deccan Horse, their bridles polished, sabres and lances held aloft.

And over the coming weeks they continued to wait, moving laboriously up to the front and back again as promises of a breakthrough came and went. But the breakthrough never came. On 18 November 1916, 140 days after the initial attack, Haig called a halt just short of the ancient burial ground of the Butte de Warlencourt. The remnants of General Sir Henry Rawlinson's 4th Army were still four miles short of Bapaume, having suffered 420,000 casualties. The passage of the fighting was charted by the unrecovered bodies and makeshift graves of 131,000 British and Empire soldiers. Over 30,000 of them had corporeally ceased to exist.

Each phase of the campaign had been costly. But the names of killing grounds such as Delville Wood, Pozières and Guillemont would not headline the battle for posterity. The Battle of the Somme, with all its doom-laden resonance, would above all be remembered for its first day.

In the early hours of a summer Saturday, a society of miners, stevedores, tramwaymen and errand boys, shipping clerks, railway porters, artists and aristocrats – along with regular and Territorial soldiers – assembled in the dirty white chalk of the British front line. They were of every age in Lord Kitchener's prescribed range of 18–40 years. Each soldier carried at least 60 lb of equipment, including a shaving kit, an iron ration, a pair of socks and a well-oiled Lee-Enfield rifle that most would never use. Those detailed to take Lewis guns, wire-cutters, rifle grenades and flares (to signal the capture of enemy trenches) carried a greater weight still. A few carried wicker baskets of carrier pigeons that later in the day a German machine-gun crew thought contained their lunch.

As dawn broke in the channel of sky above the British troops, there was only room to stand as they waited. Some small groups of men sang songs that were inaudible amid the shellfire, and cheered at the prospect of finally killing Germans. Some closed their eyes and dreamed they were elsewhere. Some shared coffee from tin helmets and dealt out chocolate and fags. Some wrote a few pencilled lines. Some stared in private reverie at their fingers pressed against the wall of earth in front of them, now drying after a midnight shower, until a wink from a neighbour said those thoughts were not theirs alone. Some prayed for their enemy as the British guns reached their climax. Most smoked. The odd man cried.

The early mist had almost gone and the sun was high enough to give warmth when the appointed moment came and, against a sky 'of the kind commonly described as heavenly', 60,000 men, in good faith and bad boots, climbed out of their trenches and advanced towards the enemy. It was 7.30 a.m. British Summer Time, 1 July 1916. Zero hour.

* * *

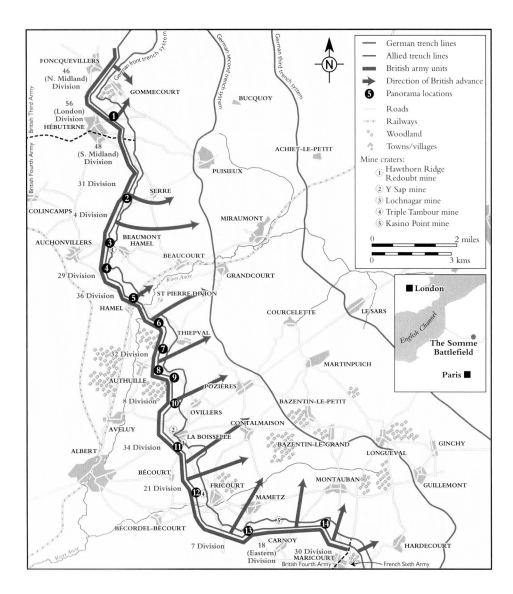

Legend:
- German trench lines
- Allied trench lines
- British army units
- Direction of British advance
- **5** Panorama locations
- Roads
- Railways
- Woodland
- Towns/villages

Mine craters:
1. Hawthorn Ridge Redoubt mine
2. Y Sap mine
3. Lochnagar mine
4. Triple Tambour mine
5. Kasino Point mine

0 ——— 2 miles
0 ——— 3 kms

Map labels:
FONCQUEVILLERS
46 (N. Midland) Division
56 (London) Division
HÉBUTERNE
GOMMECOURT
BUCQUOY
German front trench system
German second trench system
German third trench system
British Third Army
British Fourth Army
48 (S. Midland) Division
ACHIET-LE-PETIT
31 Division
PUISIEUX
SERRE
COLINCAMPS
4 Division
MIRAUMONT
AUCHONVILLERS
BEAUMONT HAMEL
BEAUCOURT
29 Division
GRANDCOURT
River Ancre
36 Division
ST PIERRE DIVION
HAMEL
THIEPVAL
COURCELETTE
LE SARS
32 Division
MARTINPUICH
AUTHUILLE
POZIÈRES
8 Division
OVILLERS
BAZENTIN-LE-PETIT
AVELUY
CONTALMAISON
LA BOISSELLE
ALBERT
34 Division
BAZENTIN-LE-GRAND
LONGUEVAL
GINCHY
BÉCOURT
FRICOURT
MONTAUBAN
21 Division
MAMETZ
GUILLEMONT
BÉCORDEL-BÉCOURT
River Ancre
7 Division
CARNOY
HARDECOURT
18 (Eastern) Division
MARICOURT
30 Division
British Fourth Army
French Sixth Army

Inset map:
London
English Channel
The Somme Battlefield
Paris

THE MAPS

All the maps in this book are based on military maps of the time. This overall map of the Somme battlefield on 1 July 1916 shows the positions of the Allied and German front lines and the direction of the British attack.

Larger-scale maps at the start of chapters show in more detail the parts of the battlefield around the fourteen individual panoramas, the positions of which are marked here.

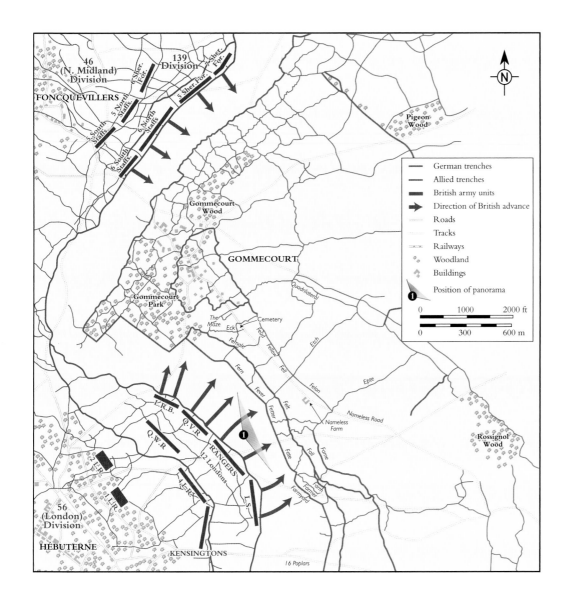

46
(N. Midland)
Division

139
Division

FONCQUEVILLERS

6 Sher. For.
5 Sher. For.
5 Sher. For.
7 Sher. For.
5 North Staffs.
6 South Staffs.
6 North Staffs.
6 South Staffs.

Pigeon
Wood

Gommecourt
Wood

GOMMECOURT

Gommecourt
Park

Quadrilateral

The
Maze
Cemetery
Eck
Fedd
Female
Fellow
Fern
Fetch
Fell
Felon
Fever
Felt
Epte

L.R.B.
Q.V.R
Q.W.R
RANGERS
12 Londons
L.R.
L.R.
M.R.
L.S.

Nameless Road
Nameless
Farm

Rossignol
Wood

Fate
Foll
Fume
Farm
Farmer
Farmyard

56
(London)
Division

HÉBUTERNE

KENSINGTONS

16 Poplars

N

	German trenches
	Allied trenches
▬	British army units
➤	Direction of British advance
	Roads
	Tracks
	Railways
	Woodland
	Buildings
1	Position of panorama

0   1000   2000 ft

0   300   600 m

Panorama No.　　　made at *c.7.30 am BST* on *c. 1st July 2015* from *W of Wood St : 12th Londons (The Rangers) 7.30 am. BST 1st July 1916*

including a field view of *149°* from about *NNW* to *SE*

Approximate Scale of Degrees (1 degree equals *1/3* inches).

GOMMECOURT

The Maze
K.46.2 . 7 1000 yds
M. G. M. G.

Ferret
530 yds

Female
630 yds

Eck
720 yds

Cemetery
K.4.d.8.7 770 yds

Fern
410 yds

Feed
530 yds

Exe
1000 yds

Feud
830 yds

Quadrilateral
K.56.3. 5 1150 yds
M. G.

Fellow
780 yds

1. Panoramas are taken solely for military purposes.
2. The publication of them in the press will necessarily give valuable information to the enemy.
3. This panorama is to be kept with as much security as is compatible with full advantage of it being taken by our own troops.
4. When troops are relieved this panorama should be handed over to the relieving troops.

12

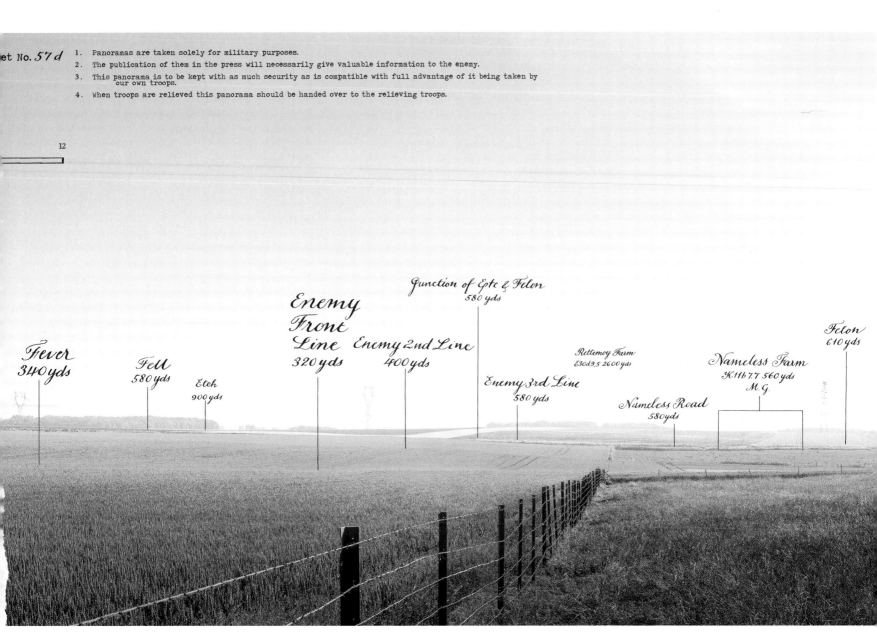

THE PANORAMAS

This book is the first narrative history of the opening day of the Battle of the Somme to include present-day panoramic photographs of the battlefield. These fourteen photographs were taken at the exact positions (shown on the map opposite) from which fourteen British battalions attacked in the first wave on that day 100 years ago. They were also taken at exactly the time of day when the attack was launched, and in near-identical weather conditions.

In the manner of the military battlefield panoramas of the time, the photographs are annotated by hand with the points of strategic significance (invariably named by the soldiers themselves) as they existed immediately before the battle.

* * *

The Great War was the first in which photography was widely used for strategic purposes. The most common of such photographs were horizontal panoramas, taken on a tripod at ground level.

Each panorama was made up of as many as 40 separate images taken in a panned sequence. When physically joined together, these gave viewers a panoramic field of view of the battlefield from the safety of their dugouts. The finished panorama included information about the location of the photographer, the date, the total field of view in degrees, the direction the camera was facing and a scale of degrees to inches.

These panoramic images were simultaneously amongst the most secret and the most numerous documents of the war. Of the 30,000 First World War military and battlefield photographs that survive to this day, 12,000 are the component parts of panoramas of this kind.

The panoramas in this book pay homage to them.

AUTHOR'S NOTE

This book is intended not as a work of academic military history, but only to tell a story. I have therefore kept notes on the text to a minimum. A list of my main published sources appears on page 135.

I have predominantly used for German trenches, German defensive positions and landmarks in German-held territory the names given to them by British soldiers, and these names appear throughout in *italics*.

Readers will notice that a set of coordinates is written below a number of the annotated place names on the panoramas. These are authentic grid references to the British military maps of the time.

While the following narrative centres on the actions in which 112 British battalions were involved on 1 July 1916, a total of 143 battalions, 142 of them British and one from the Dominions, went into battle that day. (The Dominions unit was the 1st Newfoundland Regiment, whose heroic story has been well told many times, and recently too, so I hope I may be forgiven for not re-telling it here.)

This book is dedicated to all 143 of them.

CHAPTER 1

GOMMECOURT

The village of Gommecourt was ostensibly the northernmost objective of the British offensive on 1 July, but in reality it was hardly an 'objective' at all. The attack on the village, a pincer movement involving two Territorial divisions of General Allenby's 3rd Army, was a ruse, intended to divert German resources away from the assault on the village of Serre further south. Unknown to the front-line troops, the British divisional commanders were instructed to make their intentions as obvious to the enemy as possible. The ruse failed. Confident of the strength of their Gommecourt position, the German commanders refrained from re-deploying a single soldier in its defence.

The morning of 1 July broke misty and fresh, then became cloudless and warm.[1] The 46th Division's attack at 7.30 a.m. (zero hour) over soggy, open country to the north was broken almost immediately. By 8.30 a.m., of the division's six battalions committed to the battle, only a dozen men from the 7th Sherwood Foresters had made it past the German front line.

To the south, the 56th Division advanced over similarly exposed ground. John Masefield, the future Poet Laureate, had visited the British lines at Hébuterne in the last week of June. His description of the terrain as 'open, gentle, green … a shelving, shallow hollow' is recognisable in Panorama ❶. The ground separating the two armies here, as along the whole fifteen-mile front on 1 July, had not yet been reduced to the sterile moonscape of popular memory. The outlook was still countrified. In between the shell holes, no man's land was full of thistles, hawthorn and meadowsweet. Poppies, as yet without official symbolism, grew at trench corners, and in places tall grasses grew up over the pickets and wire. As the sun rose in the thinning sky, hardly a man failed to reflect on the beauty of it. A platoon of the London Scottish felt as if they were 'starting off for a picnic'.

By the time of the attack, the London men, drawn mostly from the capital's commercial classes to replace the dead of 1915, were sleepless and exhausted. They had spent the lead-up to the battle digging. In three nights, 3,000 infantrymen made 4,500 yards of new trenches, shrinking the width of no man's land by more than half. The brigadier-general in charge had lorries full of empty biscuit tins rattle through Hébuterne to drown the noise. It was quite a feat of spadework for men whose greatest previous exertion was their daily commute. Some were to fall asleep under fire in shell holes later that afternoon.

Their work cut only the distance, however, not the odds. The Gommecourt men's role as bait rather than battle-winning soldiers had

---

1   It was 25 °C by 10.00 a.m.

PUISIEUX
4150 yds

Fate
340 yds

Fall
430 yds

Farmyard
600 yds

Farne
640 yds

Farmer
650 yds

Fair
860 yds

ol Wood
630 yds
G.

Farm
750 yds

Sunken Road
1180 yds

Sixteen Poplars
H 17a 6.8 820 yds
M. G.

BUCQUOY
4840 yds

Biez Wood
1.1a 2700yds

Felt
400 yds

Fetter
320 yds

Rossign
K12b
N

reduced their artillery support to a single spotter plane and 20 shells per gun. The preceding British bombardment had made a mess of the enemy's positions on the surface, but little impression on their underground bunkers. Seven days' shelling had killed only eight Germans. The German report for the period gives more prominence to a direct hit on one company's cooker than to casualties. Worse still for the bone-weary clerks and solicitors sharing an issue of pea soup[2] before zero hour, the British bombardment had failed to silence the Germans' heavy guns.

The assault began with smoke and whistle blasts. The whistles were barely audible and the smoke was released in such extravagant quantities that for the first 200 hundred yards the advance was completely blind. Nonetheless the leading waves initially made good progress. The wire in places was well cut and a number of defenders in the first German line readily surrendered. But within minutes, as the smoke cleared, defensive fire from the Germans' third line began to build in chaotic layers of sound. The number of British soldiers hit rose in concert with the noise. German machine-gunners emerged from their bunkers and rapidly set up their weapons in their pre-appointed spots (about 90 seconds was their drill time), while the German batteries found their rhythm and distance. Such was the intensity of the barrage back towards the British lines that for a time captured German prisoners had to be held in their own dugouts.

On the right flank, the London Scottish lost heavily but still managed to consolidate a position in *Fame* and *Fall*. The Rangers

suffered similarly while crossing no man's land. With fallen bodies already accumulating in front of him, Second Lieutenant Edward G. D. Liveing[3] went over with the 12th Londons to a 'panorama painted with three colours – the green of the grass, the white of the smoke and red of the shrapnel and blood'. The wire to the battalion's front here (from *Fetter* – where another wire fence is strung today – to *Fate*) was intact, and all four companies became targets for machine-gunners in the *Maze*, *Nameless Farm* and *Rossignol Wood*. Only about a fifth of them managed to follow the prescribed path of their attack – a half-wheel through *Fame* and along the extent of *Felon* to its junction with *Epte*. As they went, they stepped over the wounded crawling back the other way. Among them was Liveing. A machine-gun round had taken a chunk the size of a cricket ball out of his right thigh.

On the left of the attack, the Queen Victoria's Rifles' commanding officer, Lieutenant-Colonel Vernon Dickins, had watched the first waves of his men set off into the smoke 'as though they were on parade'. Cheered on by the reserve troops on either side of him, their shapes had faded, then disappeared. For two hours, Dickins heard nothing. All communication, visual and telephonic, had failed. At 9.30 a.m., a 'plucky' runner arrived with information that B and C companies had taken all their first-phase objectives (a handful of men had occupied *Fellow* and *Feud*). At Gommecourt, it was the last decent news of the day. The Queen's Westminster Rifles had followed the Vics' advance through *Fern* and *Feed*. They reached the small band of Victorias in

---

2 In a gesture of unusual largesse, the troops were also given their ration for the following day: a bacon sandwich.

3 Author of *Attack: An Infantry Subaltern's Impression of July 1st 1916* (1918), one of the first accounts of the war to be published.

Fellow. One party of men turned towards the cemetery, another towards the communication trench *Etch*, trying to bomb their way along it to the strongpoint of the *Quadrilateral*. Reduced to five subalterns and 40 men, they were forced to retreat to the cover of the sunken *Nameless Road*. To the left, the London Rifle Brigade were similarly stonewalled. In the opening minutes, they had covered the ground to *Female* with only slight casualties. Then their numbers had thinned with the smoke. They fought their way into *Eck* and the *Maze*, where they did their best to establish a position with makeshift posts and wire. Snipers picked them off from the fairground distance of the cemetery. In the days before the battle, the LRB had been told to expect only 10 per cent casualties. Just 90 minutes in, three times that number were already dead.

By 9.30 a.m., a fragile rim of London soldiers, the flotsam of the British advance, stretched from the *Maze* on the left flank to *Fair* on the right. They had obediently mimicked the arrows of the attack plan, but the arrows had got thinner and fainter with every yard. The plan had also anticipated a jubilant reunion with their northern comrades to the east of the village. But the 46th Division was nowhere to be seen.

The 46th's failure to break through the German line[4] signalled an end to the London Division's hopes. Safe from the north by 9.00 a.m., the Germans turned all their fire to their left-hand flank. Behind the Englishmen taking cover along the *Nameless Road* (now the D6 from Gommecourt to Puisieux), the ground 'boiled' with exploding shells. Ahead of them, increasing numbers of the German 2nd Guard Reserve stalked them throughout the morning below the surface, from the cemetery and up the long communication trenches from Bucquoy and Rossignol Wood. These Prussian veterans of nearly two years' fighting were old hands at close combat.[5] And while the German supplies of bombs and ammunition were close at hand, those of the British were running out. The remnants of the QWRs and QVRs searched German dugouts, blew trench blocks[6] where they could, and passed bombs and bullets from man to man to wherever the Germans were nearest. In places they resorted to waiting for German bombs, then throwing them back before they exploded. The battalion commands could do little. The front-line trenches were full of dead and wounded, and traumatised men who had already retreated. The 2nd London, 4th London and Kensingtons made heroic efforts to reinforce the forward men – the heroic efforts of soldiers who know their likely fate. Only the

---

4 From the moment when the 46th's advance faltered, corps commander Lieutenant-General 'Polar Bear' Snow had pressed the division's commander, Major-General The Hon. Edward James Montagu-Stuart-Wortley (the two had overlapped at Eton, where Snow was the junior), to send more men forward. Wortley prevaricated. He had seen 3,600 of his men lost needlessly in ten minutes at the Hohenzollern Redoubt the previous year. He would not preside over another slaughter. He reluctantly agreed to commit two companies later in the afternoon, but in the event only a single platoon went over. Of the 42 men sent forward, 41 were killed or wounded. By the end of the day, Wortley's division had sustained a total of 2,455 casualties, the smallest number of any division that attacked on 1 July. He was relieved of his command three days later.

5 A veteran of the war, Albert 'Smiler' Marshall, told the author a story in the late 1990s that bore witness to the Prussians' martial resolve. At times over the period of Albert's service, when the British and German trenches were close enough, a convention developed whereby the opposing occupants would throw each other chocolate and cigarettes attached to disabled grenades. The Bavarians apparently were particularly generous. The Prussians, on taking over the line, also threw over chocolate and cigarettes, but attached to live grenades.

6 Barriers of debris created by detonating explosives.

brave, lucky, mesmerised or faithful reached their objectives, and not enough to make a difference.

By early afternoon, desperate messages were sent to the rear. Frequently written within yards of heavily armed Germans, most of these messages observed the convention of a subordinate delivering a status report and requesting instructions. We have a cherished legacy of dead soldiers' letters to their family on the eve of battle, but the last written words of many young subalterns were not 'your ever loving', etc., but along the lines of 'Mackenzie dead. Situation serious. Only officer left.' Runners volunteered to sprint with these messages through the curtains of shellfire. Most didn't make it. Even if they did, the middle-aged officers half a mile away could offer little comfort or insight to the sender in their response. One battalion commander's best effort (addressed by this stage to 'Any officer') was to advise that an aeroplane had seen the German fourth line empty and that the recipient should occupy it forthwith: little wonder that the NCO who opened it in lieu of a superior recommended the runner carry on looking for someone with a commission. At 4.00 p.m., one officer of the London Scottish, a Captain H. C. Sparks in *Farm* (where the German pressure was greatest), was waiting no longer for battalion HQ: 'I am faced with this position,' his communiqué read; 'I have collected all bombs and SAA [small arms ammunition] from casualties. Every one has been used. I am faced with three alternatives: A. To stay here with such of my men as are alive and be killed. B. To surrender to the enemy. C. To withdraw such men as I can. Either of these first two alternatives is distasteful to me. I propose to adopt the latter.' He led a fighting retreat with a handful of his men from shell hole to shell hole through *Farmer* and *Farmyard* and reached the British lines after dark.

Most pockets of Londoners along the front now chose to head backwards without recording their decision. Their early successes had cost them dearly. It was a long way back. On the right, the enemy now had a free hand from *Fair* to *Fame*. A shallow tide of beleaguered soldiers therefore now ebbed northwestwards, in most cases withdrawing in a rearguard action. While his adopted band of Westminsters made their escape, one wounded officer of the 5th Cheshire Pioneers, a Lieutenant G. S. Arthur, held off a platoon of German bombers in *Exe* for twenty minutes unarmed. He finally couldn't return their grenades fast enough. Similar acts of self-sacrifice allowed the now hybrid groups of men to straggle in stages back towards the German front line. Many shared temporary shelters with the day's wounded along the way, both English and German. A Private Schuman rolled into a crater on top of a German soldier. An abandoned prisoner, the man had been severely mutilated by a German shell. 'Schlecht, schlecht, [bad, bad]' were the man's only words. Schuman took his hand, squeezed it and carried on his way.

Edward Liveing was one casualty who earlier in the day had succeeded in returning to the British lines. Wounded between *Fate* and *Fall*, he had crawled to and over the *Sunken Road* (now the D27 from Hébuterne to Puisieux). Assisted by a sergeant and his platoon observer, he made it across the final yards of no man's land and plunged into Woman Street, hovering on the edge of consciousness. His tunic and breeches were shredded with shrapnel and bullet holes and soaked purple with blood. There he found a signaller sat in a wrecked dugout, calmly transmitting messages to battalion headquarters. A gunner colonel stood outside. 'Good morning,' the colonel said, lowering his field glasses. 'Good morning, sir,' Liveing replied. 'Where are you hit?' the colonel asked. Liveing replied it was not serious. 'Good,' said the colonel, once again raising his field glasses; 'How are we getting on?'

By early evening, the last of the London Rifle Brigade in *Eck* had been forced to retire to *Ferret*. All remnants of the neighbouring battalions now joined them. At 8.30 p.m., only five officers and 70 men remained. Until now all had acted as members of the British Army. The time had now come for them to act independently. The order 'Every man for himself' was shouted over the din. A cabal of German snipers in *Eck* was lined up on the British position. In stages, the survivors of the day made a bolt for it like clays from a trap. Some escaped. Some were hit. Some fell 'dead, dying, wounded, feigning death – who knows?'[7] The battle was over.

As the sun set behind Hébuterne, a thin haze hung over the battlefield. It was now a junkyard of tangled wire, ordnance, equipment and bodies. Heavy artillery and machine guns fired only intermittently. The cries of the wounded became audible. A German leutnant gave permission to a British officer bearing a white flag in his sector to recover them: both officers agreed to inform only their front-line men.[8] Some Germans helped carry wounded British soldiers back to the British lines.

From the seven battalions of the 56th Division that had attacked (6,200 soldiers), over 1,700 men were dead; some 200 (mainly wounded) were prisoners of war, and 2,300 were wounded, mostly now lying between the British lines and the *Nameless Road*. The London Scottish had suffered 616 casualties from 871 men committed to the battle. Of the London Rifle Brigade's 248 dead, 80 per cent have no known grave. On the German side, fewer than 1,400 men were killed or wounded, and the Gommecourt Salient still thrust out as far into the British front as it had that morning. As dusk fell, the division's commander, Major-General Charles Amyatt Hull, walked back with his adjutant from his vantage point over the battlefield to his quarters at Mailly Maillet. He never spoke a word.

Gommecourt remained in German hands for the next eight months. When the 31st and 46th divisions reoccupied the village on the night of 27 February 1917, they found the skeletons of British soldiers still hanging on the German wire.

* * *

The cemetery seen in Panorama ❶ is Gommecourt British Cemetery No. 2: 1,357 men are buried here, many of them soldiers from the 56th Division. Among them are two brothers, Rifleman Henry Edward Bassett, aged 25, and Rifleman Philip James Bassett, aged 20, both killed on 1 July. They are buried side by side.

---

7   The words of Private Schuman.

8   Truces or fraternisation of any kind were strictly forbidden by the German and the British commands.

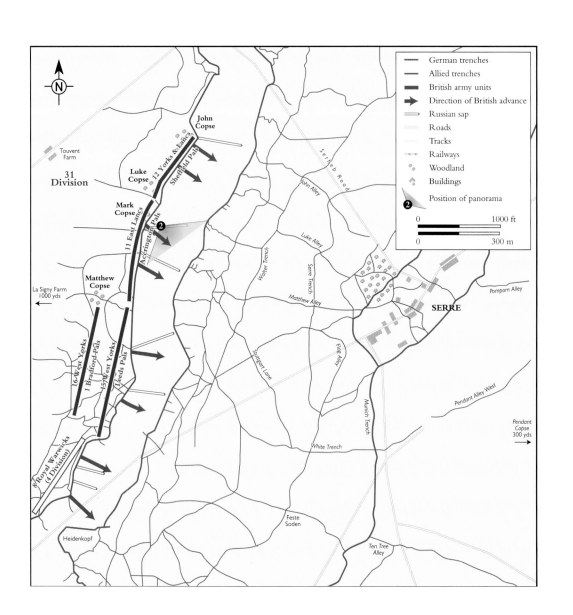

German trenches
Allied trenches
British army units
Direction of British advance
Russian sap
Roads
Tracks
Railways
Woodland
Buildings
Position of panorama

0 ——— 1000 ft
0 ——— 300 m

N

Touvent
Farm

**31
Division**

John
Copse

Luke
Copse

12 Yorks & Lancs
Sheffield Pals

Mark
Copse

11 East Lancs

Accrington Pals

Matthew
Copse

La Signy Farm
1000 yds

16 West Yorks
1 Bradford Pals
15 West Yorks
Leeds Pals

8 Royal Warwicks
(4 Division)

Heidenkopf

Serre b Road

John Alley

Luke Alley

Wolter Trench

Serre Trench

Matthew Alley

Stuttgart Lane

Flag Alley

White Trench

Munich Trench

Feste
Soden

Ten Tree
Alley

SERRE

Pompom Alley

Pendant Alley West

Pendant
Copse
300 yds

CHAPTER 2

SERRE

'Two years in the making. Ten minutes in the destroying. That was our history.' These famous last words of John Harris's 1961 novel *Covenant with Death* grimly summarise the fate of one division's attack on 1 July. The division was the 31st, comprising the volunteer 'Pals' battalions from Yorkshire, Lancashire and Durham; the objective of the attack was the small village of Serre.

The ground here had already been bitterly fought over the year before. In June 1915, General de Castelnau's 2nd French Army had attacked the German positions straddling the hilltop farms of Toutvent and La Signy. After a week of reckless bravery, the French *poilus* had failed to take Serre, but had forced the Germans back to a treeless ridge just 1,000 yards from the village. The French took over the vacated German trenches 300 yards further down the slope. It was to this line of captured trenches that the British came in December 1915, and from it that they would attack seven months later. To their backs were four freestanding copses of oak trees named after the Gospels; to their front was a silhouetted, skullcap-shaped hill.

The assault on Serre was the northern wing of the main British offensive. For General Haig, this was where the battle was to start, but not where it would be won. The role of the men on this left-hand boundary would be primarily protective. With John Copse as its axis, an orderly phalanx of soldiers would execute a left-hand 90-degree turn through the village and form a shield to the British advance's exposed northeastern flank. The 31st Division was chosen for what the top brass deemed to be this simple manoeuvre.

At the outbreak of war, the northern 'Pals' had been amongst the first to rush to the colours. For many with an appreciable stake in the fruits of Empire, the appeals to enlist could wait. For the men of the poorer industrial centres such as Leeds, Bradford, Barnsley and Halifax, Lord Kitchener's pointing finger (in the famous recruiting poster of the time) promised glory and adventure beyond the mill or pit. It also offered £1 1s a week. Yet these small,[1] flat-capped men were impressed less by the pay than by the guarantee that came with it: those that enlisted together would fight together. They joined the queues to swear an oath to the king because they knew they would stay with their friends. The prospect of a uniform and a brotherhood – and a pride in both that most had never known before – made them smile and wave while they did it.

---

1 An often overlooked detail of the Great War is that those who fought in it were considerably smaller than we are today. In 2014, the average height of an adult British man was 5 ft 9 in. In 1914, it was 5 ft 6 in, and the average height of men from the poorer industrial north was less still.

7d

1916

1. Panoramas are taken solely for military purposes.
2. The publication of them in the press will necessarily give valuable information to the enemy.
3. This panorama is to be kept with as much security as is compatible with full advantage of it being taken by our own troops.
4. When troops are relieved this panorama should be handed over to the relieving troops.

12

E

Trench
ds

630 yds

M.G
K29b83.24 430 yds

Pendant Copse
131a 6.7 2000 yds

Matthew Alley
500 yds

Pendant Alley West
1230 yds

Walter Trench
400 yds

M.G
K30c21.18 870 yds

Ten Tree Alley
1500 yds

Stuttgart Lane
360 yds

FOURTH ARMY.

Panorama No. *2* made at *c.7.30 am. BST* on *c.1st July 2015* from *E of Mark Copse: 11th East Lancashire Regiment (Accrington Pals) 7.30a*

including a field view of *112°* from about *ENE* to *SSW*

Approximate Scale of Degrees (1 degree equals *2/5* inches).

0   1   2   3   4   5   6   7   8   9   10

M.G
K.23d 72.20 480 yds

M.G.
K.29b 55.69 280 yds

Serheb Road
760 yds

John Alley
700 yds

Luke Alley
500 yds

Pompom Alley
1400 yds

S   E

M.G
K.29b 82.43 430 y

It had been a long journey from the recruiting office to the Somme, via makeshift camps on windswept moors, coastal trenches[2] and the banks of the Suez Canal. For two years they had endured the brutal and archaic rituals of a still Victorian army. Now the moment they had longed for and dreaded had come.

On the evening of 30 June, the 31st Division began the seven-mile march from their billets to the front line. The remaining French villagers looked on in silence. The soldiers were mostly silent too. 'The feeling of comradeship among us seemed to grow as we marched forward into a common danger,' recalled Private W. Slater of the 2nd Bradford Pals. 'In particular, I have a lasting memory of the man who was closest to me as we marched. I was only eighteen at the time, having joined the army under age, and he was some years older than I. As he spoke to me I became aware of a feeling almost of tenderness in him towards me, as though he sensed my fears and was trying to reassure both himself and me. "Don't worry, Bill," he said. "We'll be all right." And he spoke as gently as a mother trying to soothe a frightened child.'

They stopped halfway and were given tea and bars of chocolate. The addition of a sausage was thought so incongruous that most men refused to eat it. They thought it had been drugged to steady their nerves. As they passed the small hollow of Basin Wood, they saw pioneer soldiers digging a mass grave.

In his eve-of-battle oration, the commander of VIII Corps, General Aylmer Hunter-Weston, had told the troops that they would 'walk' into Serre. The German wire had been 'blown to hell', he said. Now, however, from their forward positions the troops could see it 'standing strong and well'. As skylarks in what remained of the four copses behind them signalled dawn, each battalion received its final instructions. The men had drawn some comfort from the assumption that they would go forward in semi-darkness. They were now told they were to attack in full daylight. There was to be no turning back. Every man was to advance at a steady pace. No fighting soldier was to stop and help the wounded. They were assured of the importance of the battle, the nobility of the cause and the likelihood of victory. They were also reminded of Point 13 of the Operation Order: any man stopping or trying to turn back would be shot.

Like the finale to a firework display, at 7.20 a.m. the week-long British bombardment began its final 10-minute hurricane. The result was deafening. A man shouting into the ear of the man next to him could not be heard. Sergeant Charles Moss of the 18th Durham Light Infantry (DLI) compared the fountains of smoke and chalk to the 'heavy seas roaring and rolling' onto the Hendon beaches during the winter storms of his last leave. Under cover of the barrage, the men of the leading waves crawled out into no man's land to their jump-off positions within 200 yards of the German front line, the so-called 'shilling seats'.[3]

At 7.30 a.m. exactly, as if to the hand-pinch of a conductor, the guns stopped, giving way to one of the great silences of history. As the British

---

2 England had its trenches too. The 18th Durham Light Infantry manned the Tyne and Tees defences over the war's first winter. On the morning of 16 December 1914, six of its men were killed by shellfire from three German battle-cruisers during Admiral von Hipper's raid on Hartlepool. They were the first of Kitchener's New Army to be killed in action.

3 So called after the seats in a theatre closest to the stage. Panorama ❷ is taken from the 'shilling seats' of the Accrington Pals.

Fold out for Panorama ❷: *Serre*

gun-layers adjusted their sights to the next German line, only the sounds of nature could be heard. For some it offered the momentary illusion of a cathartic last-minute reprieve. Lieutenant Asquith of the 1st Barnsley Pals was almost disappointed. 'It's a walk-over,' he told his waiting troops.

Sergeant Moss, however, foresaw no such anti-climax. Through the clearing smoke, he could see shirtsleeved German soldiers on the horizon carrying up machine guns and ammunition. Like a boxer waiting on the ropes for his opponent to punch himself out, the German artillery had bided its time. At a signal of red flares from the German front line, it now laid down a barrage of its own. Carefully measured stripes of shellfire fell from no-man's land through to the well-observed British reserve lines. The explosions looked like 'a thick belt of poplar trees'.

As the leading British waves advanced, the smoky air was torn with shrapnel shells and machine-gun rounds. With their rifles slung around their necks and 'having done with all pleasant things', the British troops walked forward into the maelstrom. Struggling to get to their feet under the weight of their equipment, many died on their knees. Forming up in their prescribed order (two to three yards apart), whole lines of soldiers were cut down within seconds. Men fell in sequence – some sinking slowly, others throwing up their hands – on the cue of a traversing machine gun. Private Reginald Glenn of the Sheffield Pals saw his comrades go down so quickly that he assumed their orders had been changed; instead of being told to walk, he thought they must now have been told to lie down. In the chaos, men looked to their officers. News of their being hit was passed, man to man, down the line.

Scores of the leading men fell only yards beyond the British trenches. An even greater number were hit without getting that far. The 1st Barnsley and 1st and 2nd Bradford Pals, starting from behind the front line, sustained almost 40 per cent casualties before even reaching it. For many of the civilian soldiers, it was their first experience of the effects of high explosive. As Lance Corporal Fred Sayer waited in front of Mark Copse to go over, a shell burst in the Accringtons' trench. Recovering his senses, Sayer found the three men next to him were dead. The first, evidently killed by concussion, still sat quietly with no visible mark; the second, apparently buried, stood upright on his severed waist. Sayer had to deduce the fate of the third from the blood and residues of flesh on his own equipment. Sergeant Moss passed a man carrying his right forearm. 'Why have they done this to me? I've never done anything to them,' the man said.

From the moment when their distant rattle had broken the silence at zero hour, the German machine guns in Gommecourt and Rossignol Wood[4] to the left of the Sheffields and Accringtons had accounted for most of their casualties. The descending bullets raked the ground with the sound of 'heavy rain'. Within another 90 seconds, the men of the German 8th Baden Infanterie had set up no fewer than ten more guns to their front.[5]

---

4   Readers would be forgiven for suspecting a misprint here. Gommecourt and Rossignol Wood were more than 3,000 yards away (they appear in Panorama ❶). Yet this was well within the range of First World War machine guns (the German M 08 had a maximum range of 3,828 yards; the British Vickers, 4,500) and they were frequently used at this distance. Machine guns were fired in bursts. The bullets did not follow precisely the same trajectory but instead formed a 'cone of fire' which translated into an elliptical 'beaten zone' on the ground over which enemy troops were attacking. Machine guns were therefore often used in effect as artillery pieces to lay down barrages.

5   High up in the historic machine-gun hall of fame, at least six of these ten machine guns were given names by the Germans, in some cases the names of their operators. The names (with corresponding map references) were Wilhelm (K23d72.20), Adelbrecht (K29b55.69), Kolle (K29b82.43), Schumann (K30a24.31), Spengler (K29b83.24) and Kaiser (K29b21.22): all are marked on Panorama ❷.

Enemy Second Line
550 yds

Enemy Front Line
550 yds

Frontier Line
1800 yds

British Front Line : The Leeds Pals
550 yds

The Heidenkopf
K.35.a.3.2
1000 yds

Tormented in their bunkers for the last seven days, the German machine-gun crews now followed their rehearsed routine with frenzied precision. Each emplacement was carefully positioned. Their interlocking fields of fire created geometric killing grounds across the whole front. Musketier Karl Blenk soon found such calculations unnecessary: 'We were very surprised to see them walking … I saw one of the officers walking calmly, carrying a walking stick. When we started firing, we just had to reload and reload. They went down in the hundreds. You didn't have to aim, we just fired into them.' At a rate of 500 rounds a minute, belt after 250-round belt was relentlessly emptied into the British lines. 'Skin hung in ribbons from the fingers of the *Schützen* [shooters] and the gun commanders,' recorded Unteroffizier Otto Lais. The constant pressure on trigger thumbs turned them into 'swollen, shapeless lumps of flesh'. Guns jammed through overheating. German gunners urinated into their cooling jackets. MG Adelbrecht had fired 12,000 rounds before Unteroffizier Adelbrecht himself was shot in the head. The weapon stationed on the Serre–Mailly Road (K35b11.77) had fired 20,000 by the end of the battle.

Second Lieutenant T. Reilly of the Royal Field Artillery watched the scene from an observation post 300 yards behind the British lines. 'The machine guns and their gunners were clearly visible, but all our guns were in the main barrage and were not to be brought back, except by order of VIII Corps H.Q.' He looked on helplessly as the guns that had lifted from the enemy's front three lines at zero hour now extended their range still further away from the battle.

Within ten minutes of going over, the British attack had faltered irretrievably. After half an hour, the battle was as good as over. Yet to Brigadier-General Hubert Conway Rees, the commanding officer of 94th Brigade, at his advance HQ 500 yards behind Mark Copse, the fate of his troops was still unknown. All lines of communication with company commanders had failed. Shiny triangles cut from biscuit tins had been sewn on to the back of the assaulting troops' tunics. Their reflection was intended to show the extent of the advance,[6] but the battlefield was shrouded in smoke. The succeeding waves of British soldiers were therefore permitted to walk forward into the firestorm.

Unteroffizier Otto Lais watched them come: 'Those that followed took cover behind their dead, groaning and moaning comrades … they shot at us as if possessed, without taking much aim. [There were] many hanging, fatally wounded, whimpering in the remnants of the wire entanglements.' The agents of mutilating injury were not limited to machine guns, shells and grenades: 'Two Minenwerfer still fired somehow in the sector and a makeshift mortar constructed by the Pioniers, a so-called Albrechtsmörser … this sent its shaky "Marmalade bucket" filled with a high explosive charge, iron and thick glass, swaying through the air. When one such monster exploded 3 to 4 metres above the ground, the results were terrible to see.'

The slaughter in no man's land was observed by fellow Britons not only from behind their lines but also from in front of them. In the lead-up to the battle, 2,000 tunnellers had dug a number of Russian saps[7] out from the

---

6 With the sun in the east, these triangles made better targets for the Germans than signals for the British.

British lines to within, in places, fifteen yards of the German front trenches. In the event, however, divisional commanders could not agree on what to do with them, and not a single sap was used. Tunnelling officers crouched alone in the sap-heads. They beckoned runners and reinforcements to come and share their cover, but in the clamour of the battle they could not be heard.

Given that, within the first hour of the attack, the British soldiers at Serre had advanced into more than 100,000 rounds of ammunition as well as many hundreds of shells and grenades, it is astonishing that any of them passed the enemy front line. Some did, however. Ten Sheffield soldiers breached a German second-line trench in front of the Serheb Road. A Private Fretwell survived being hit in the face with a grenade; the panicked German soldier had neglected to remove the pin. A party of Accringtons traded bombs with the third line below *Matthew Alley*, where the Germans had in shock initially raised their hands to surrender before thinking better of it. But the day's greatest feat of gallantry belonged to another group of the 11th East Lancs and a dozen men from the 18th DLI. Against a whole garrison of trained professional soldiers, this small group, whose names will never be known, struggled into Serre itself. The DLI men got as far as *Pendant Copse*. None were seen again.[8]

The disaster was on such a scale that by late morning all efforts were transferred to establishing defensive positions in the wrecked British front line. An enemy counter-attack was reported to be imminent. But the Germans were exhausted too. No longer firing for their survival, they now sniped at the wounded, even at the dead. A Lieutenant Heptonstall watched the corpse of an Accrington soldier propped against the German wire: 'He was sniped at during the day until his head was completely shot away.'

In front of the Gospel Copses, an area of 300 by 700 yards was covered with more than 2,000 dead or wounded North Country soldiers.[9] A German patrol that night recovered a Lewis gun, a large number of rifles and a severely wounded Accrington man whom they brought in for treatment. They also recovered a sack of mail brought forward in the attack, containing letters postmarked 'Barnsley'.

In his special order of the day, Brigadier-General Rees wrote: 'I have been through many battles in this war, and nothing more magnificent has come to my notice. The waves went forward as if on drill parade and I saw no man turn back or falter.'

The German report on the enemy and the battle was shorter: 'Sehr haben sie Gekriegt aber nicht Serre.' They had much, but they did not have Serre.

* * *

The cemetery nearest the camera in Panorama ❷ is Queen's Cemetery, in which 311 British soldiers are buried. They are mostly men of the Accrington Pals killed on 1 July. Their bodies were not recovered from the battlefield on which the cemetery stands until May 1917. The cemetery to the right is Serre Road No. 3 Cemetery. Most of the 81 graves here belong to Leeds Pals, buried in the ground over which they attacked.

7   Narrow trenches dug just below the surface of the ground to give cover to advancing troops, so called due to their widespread use in the Crimean War (1853–6).

8   When the Germans abandoned Serre in February 1917, soldiers' remains were found bearing brass shoulder insignia reading 'East Lancashire'.

9   Of a total of 3,599 casualties the 31st Division suffered on 1 July.

Smoke Trench
920 yds

Rump Trench
770 yds

Steak Line
680 yds

B E A U M O I

Coke Trench
730 yds

B E A U C O U R T - S U R - A N

Artillery Lane
2500 yds

Beaumont Alley
1100 yds

*Enemy
Front
Line*
250 yds

Quarry Po
Q11 a 8.9 78

FOURTH ARMY.

Map Sheet No. *57d*

1. P
2. T
3. T
4. W

Panorama No. *3* made at *c.7.30a.m. B.S T* on *c.1st July 2015* from *End of the Sunken Lane: 1st Lancs Fusiliers 7.30 a.m. B.S T 1st July 1916*

including a field view of *110°* from about **NE** to **SSE**

Approximate Scale of Degrees (1 degree equals *2/5* inches).

0   1   2   3   4   5   6   7   8   9   10

M.G.
Q5 c 23,79 450 yds

Frontier Line
650 yds

M.G
Q5 c 25,71 420 yds

Wagon Road
1100 yds

The Lynchet
80 yds

Enemy Front Line
250 yds

BERGWERK
Q5 c 6,7 540 yds
M.G

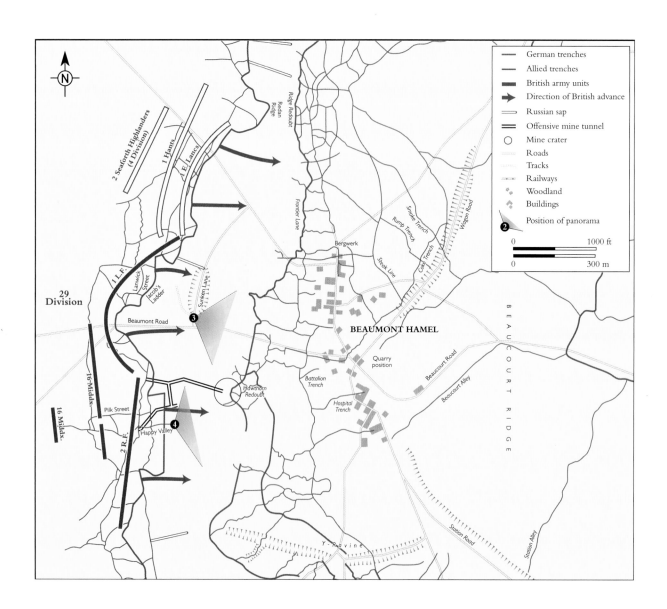

Legend:

- German trenches
- Allied trenches
- British army units
- Direction of British advance
- Russian sap
- Offensive mine tunnel
- Mine crater
- Roads
- Tracks
- Railways
- Woodland
- Buildings
- ❷ Position of panorama

0   1000 ft

0   300 m

N

2 Seaforth Highlanders (4 Division)

1 Hants.

A E I Lancs.

1 L.F.

Lanwick Street

Jacob's Ladder

29 Division

Beaumont Road

Sunken Lane

❸

16 Middx.

Pilk Street

16 Middx.

2 R.F.

Happy Valley

❹

Hawthorn Redoubt

Ridge Redoubt

Redan Ridge

Frontier Lane

Smoke Trench

Rump Trench

Steak Line

Bergwerk

Cade Trench

Wagon Road

BEAUMONT HAMEL

Quarry position

Battalion Trench

Hospital Trench

Beaucourt Road

Beaucourt Alley

B E A U C O U R T   R I D G E

Station Road

Station Alley

Y - Ravine

CHAPTER 3

BEAUMONT HAMEL & HAWTHORN RIDGE

The Somme was not the first battle in which young men died in their helpless thousands, but it was the first in which their death was captured on film.

By the beginning of the twentieth century, the British people were used to seeing each other in photographs. The sharing of snaps of children, football teams or trips to the seaside was a new social medium: Instagram on small sepia squares. By 1914, the moving picture show was also a popular staple, with 4,000 lavish 'picture palaces' selling 20 million tickets a week. As well as Charlie Chaplin comedies and Hollywood dramas, the nightly fare included newsreels. At the start of the war, British cinema audiences therefore expected to see news of the fighting, but they were to be disappointed. Under the Defence of the Realm Act, all news reports from the front were censored under Lord Kitchener's instructions. Correspondents and cameramen were allowed to operate in France, but only with official permission, and all requests to film at the front were refused.

But while the British people's support for the war was almost universal, neutral nations had to be won over. It was gradually conceded that moving pictures had a key part to play in this propaganda war. In October 1915, the government's top-secret Wellington House Committee finally authorised two cameramen to go to France. Geoffrey Malins worked for Gaumont, and Edward Tong for Jury's Imperial

Pictures. Together they made a number of films over the winter and spring, but none really captured the public. What was needed was an epic. In June 1916, Tong was invalided home and replaced by John Benjamin 'Mac' MacDowell, a director of the British and Colonial Kinematograph Company. On 24 June 1916, Malins and MacDowell arrived on the Somme.

Between 25 and 29 June, the two men filmed the final preparations for the battle as the legions of troops and machines made their way to the front. On the 30th, Malins was despatched to the British sector in front of Beaumont Hamel, a German-held village in the cleft of a valley north of the Ancre. There he would film one of the showpieces of 1 July: the detonation of 40,600 lb mine (known as H3) under the German stronghold on Hawthorn Ridge.

At the beginning of the war, the British had lagged significantly behind the Germans in tunnel warfare. One eccentric millionaire and Liverpool football fan made sure they caught up. Born in 1871, the son of a Somerset building surveyor, John Norton-Griffiths had made a fortune from digging the Manchester sewers. In February 1915, he persuaded Kitchener to allow his digging teams to be formed into the first units of the Royal Engineer tunnelling companies. When Kitchener demanded 10,000 more of his 'moles', Norton-Griffiths toured industrial Britain in his battered Rolls-Royce, recruiting the pick of the nation's

HAWTHORN REDOUBT
Q10b7.7 360yds

M.G.
Q10b75.69 390yds

M.G.
Q10b83.72
440yds

M.G.
Q10b71.81 340yds

Y Ravine
920yds

MMEL

Church
630yds

Hardwick Trench
1380 yds

Tank Alley
1300 yds

Station Alley
1350 yds

Station Road
M Gs

Cemetery
Q11 d 17. 75

Quarry
Q11d 55. 28 1600yds

Battalion
430yds

Enemy
Front
Line
310yds

miners. They would soon outpace the enemy tunnellers by four times – digging, in nine-inch increments, up to nearly nine yards a day.

The shaft of the tunnel towards the German salient on Hawthorn Ridge was sunk near Pilk Street in November 1915. The gallery was to be dug a distance of nearly 400 yards at a depth of 75 feet. Working in 6- or 12-hour shifts, the Welsh and Cornish miners of the 252nd Tunnelling Company, together with their canaries,[1] slowly and silently picked their way through the unyielding Picardy chalk. It was a filthy and unnerving business. The slightest sound from a single clumsy scrape or dropped grafting tool risked their being buried, alive or dead, by the detonation of an enemy counter-charge. For the last 150 feet, the chalk was softened with water and prised out with bayonets. The spoil was camouflaged on the surface by fast-growing cress and mustard seeds. By early June 1916, the gallery had reached its objective, and in the early hours of 27 June, 1,600 petrol cans full of ammonal explosive were wheeled on trollies under the German redoubt. On the morning of 1 July, they would make the loudest man-made sound in history.[2]

Beaumont Hamel was one of the most robustly defended villages on the whole battlefront, 'a fortress and a masterwork of German brainwork, spadework and ironwork', as the celebrated First World War poet Edmund Blunden recorded. Facing it were two regular army battalions of the 'Incomparable' 29th Division: the 1st Lancashire Fusiliers on the left in front of the village, and the 2nd Royal Fusiliers to the right on the plateau of Hawthorn Ridge. The high-achieving public-schoolboy volunteers of the 16th Middlesex supported them.[3]

Major-General Sir Henry de Beauvoir de Lisle, commander of the 29th Division, had intended to address his men on 28 June but postponed doing so due to heavy rain. He spoke to them in tolerable sunshine on the morning of the 30th instead, from the seat of a prancing horse: 'I cannot allow the battalion of which I'm so proud to enter this great battle without coming to wish you good luck, and to give you the general situation.' He offered encouragement by saying that if all the 40,000 tonnes of shells fired at the enemy on their Corps front were loaded into lorries, they would create a 46-mile traffic jam. Malins filmed the scene. The general's words 'thrilled the hearts of everyone who heard them', his memoirs recorded, and the men's faces 'shone with a new light'. In the film you can't see the men's faces, nor that a number of soldiers were afterwards disciplined by their officers for mutters of bitter dissent.

In front of the village, 450 yards separated the British and German front lines. To cut the distance by half, in the weeks before the battle British patrols had taken control of a sunken lane that ran northwards up the slope from the Beaumont Road. The forward 1st Lancs men would use it as their jump-off point at zero hour. It was here that Malins came an hour before the attack on the morning of 1 July and took some

---

1 These so-called 'miner's friends' were issued to the tunnelling companies as an official item. Their acute susceptibility to gas warned miners to evacuate a mine shaft before levels became dangerous. Many of the birds died, but others would recover on the surface. At least one company allowed a bird that had survived three gassings to be pensioned off to an aviary.

2 The record was held for only eight minutes. At 7.28 a.m., the mine at La Boisselle would make a louder noise still.

3 The battalion's sporting talent enabled it to field two Rugby Union teams and one Association Football team, made up entirely of international players.

of the most powerful images of the war. They record the faces of men who knew they had a 50 per cent chance (they had done their sums) of being killed or mutilated in the next two hours.

At 6.30 a.m., Malins left them to their futures and made his way back towards the British front line. Behind it, from a vantage point near a stepped trench known as Jacob's Ladder, he made ready. He had been told to be ten minutes early.

While the eighteen other mines laid under the German lines on the Somme front were scheduled to blow up at 7.28 a.m., there had been some disagreement over the timing of H3. General Aylmer Hunter-Weston, the commander of VIII Corps, wanted the mine blown at 3.30 a.m. to allow time for his troops to consolidate the crater. The Inspector of Mines demurred: British troops had a poor record of occupying craters before the enemy, and he recommended the explosion should coincide with the moment of the British advance. In consultation with 4th Army HQ, a compromise time of 7.20 a.m. was agreed. It would be one of the most fatal decisions by committee in history.

At 7.19 a.m. and 30 seconds, Malins began to hand-crank his Moy & Bastie camera. The chain and cogs turned. Major-General de Lisle's Fusiliers on the Hawthorn plateau waited, all eyes fixed on the ridge. The film was exposed at 16 frames per second; the magazine contained only 400 ft of film and was running low. 'Would it go up before I had time to reload? … The agony was awful, indescribable. My hand began to shake.' Then the mine blew.

It exploded with a detonation velocity of 9,842 miles an hour. Over 40 German soldiers were immolated. A great sponge of smoke and earth rose over 1,000 feet in the air. Malins gripped his tripod to stay upright. The shock waves knocked over some men in the 2nd Fusiliers front line. The crater was 165 feet wide and 70 feet deep, and the chalk debris that appeared like a 'giant snowstorm' took over a minute to subside.

Rocks were still falling as the German defenders, some with perforated eardrums, reached the 18-foot high lip of the crater. Down below, other German troops from Reserve Infanterie Regiment 119 had manned their positions opposite the Sunken Lane. They could do so in almost absolute safety. In line with the revised plan, the VIII Corps heavy artillery barrage had lifted at the moment the mine was detonated.[4] When the British subalterns blew their whistles, German thumbs were already pressed white on the triggers of their machine guns.

At 7.25 a.m., the advance waves of 2nd Royal Fusiliers sprinted towards the great white mound of the crater. It was the race of their lives. Begun five minutes after the starter pistol, it was also a race that over 300 men would lose before they got to the German wire. Machine guns on their right flank, particularly one above Y-Ravine (with map reference Q11c55.68, on Panorama ❷) operated by Unteroffizier Boehme, cut down the City of London professionals in enfiladed clumps.

At the foot of the hill, the more sedate advance of the Lancashire men (they walked) had proved costlier still. At Serre, the German machine-gunners fired approximately 10,000 rounds each. In front of

---

4 The early detonation of the mine and the corresponding lift in artillery spelled doom not only for VIII Corps. The explosion was so loud and its significance so clear that the defenders were alerted to the imminent attack for several miles along the front.

d

1. Panoramas are taken solely for military purposes.

2. The publication of them in the press will necessarily give valuable information to the enemy.

3. This panorama is to be kept with as much security as is compatible with full advantage of it being taken by our own troops.

4. When troops are relieved this panorama should be handed over to the relieving troops.

12

M.G.
72 450 yds

M.G.
Q10b 92.70 470 yds

Enemy Front Line
400 yds

B E A U M O N

B   E   A   U   C   O   U   R

M.G.
Q5d 79.69 1540 yds

M.G.
Q6c 10.70 1640 yds

Panorama No. *4* made at *c.7.30 am. BST* on *c.1st July 2015* from *End of Happy Valley: 2nd Royal Fusiliers 7.30 am. BST 1st July*

including a field view of *135°* from about **N N E** to **S S E**

Approximate Scale of Degrees (1 degree equals *1/3* inches).

0   1   2   3   4   5   6   7   8   9   10

M.G.
Q 106 75.69 450 yds

H A W T H O R N   R E D

M.G
Q 106 71.81 400 yds

BERGWERK
Q 5 c 6.7 700 yds

R E D A N   R I D G E

British Front Line
1st East Lancs
1300 yds

Ridge Redoubt
M.Gs
Enemy Front Line
1300 yds

Beaumont Hamel, no emplacement fired more than 3,000. After less than twelve belts of ammunition, there were simply no targets left. On exiting the Sunken Lane, the Fusiliers' extended order was devastatingly enfiladed by a machine gun just behind the crater (map reference Q10b75.69, on Panoramas ❸ and ❹). Of the leading waves, only 50 men got as far as the Lynchet.[5] A handful of men got further, including two officers with drawn swords. None reached the wire. Heavy-calibre bullets cut some in half at close range.

Corporal George Ashurst was one of a group of bombers who, advancing from Lanwick Street, had dived for cover into the Sunken Lane. 'Picking myself up, and looking around, my God, what a sight! The whole of the road was strewn with dead and dying men. Some were talking deliriously, others calling for help and water.' One of them with a shoulder missing caught Ashurst's eye as he passed. 'Go on, Corporal, get the bastards!' he said.

Ashurst and his fellow bombers made an improvised charge. 'Run – that was the only thing in my mind. Run and dodge. Expecting at any second to get hit, to feel a bullet hit me, I was zig-zagging, holding my head down so a bullet would hit my tin hat … You could hear when a bullet hit somebody, you could hear it hit him! Hear him groan and go down … I ran on and there was nobody with me, I was by myself, so I got a bit frightened then. When I came across this shell hole I dropped in it. I could look back over our lines. I could see our wounded, they would get up and try to go on and then they'd drop; they'd been shot again.'

Forty Royal Fusiliers made it into the crater. Bayoneting a German sentry, they caught a section of a defending platoon still in their dugout. A British officer brandishing grenades demanded surrender and was shot in the face with a flare. Two German platoons (120 men) soon arrived from depth positions with a pair of light machine guns. A machine-gun firefight now ensued across the crater at a distance of 60 yards, during which a Royal Flying Corps plane dropped bombs (to little effect) on the defenders. Outgunned and unreinforced, the remaining Fusiliers now retreated. Corporal Ashurst took their withdrawal as his cue: 'I didn't know what they were doing, but I thought, "Jerry's counter-attacking … if he comes over the top here, I'm for it all right" … so I made my mind up that I'd got to move and move very quick. I got up and dashed down this slope again and dived into the Sunken Road once more. Safe again – they'd missed again!'

At 8.00 a.m., the 16th Middlesex advanced along the ridge above the Beaumont Road. From his position on the opposite bank, Malins captured the moment. In the grainy, flickering frames, three microscopic men can be seen to fall.[6] In close-up reality, the soldiers had collapsed, either maimed or dead, under the ballistic trauma of a 0.311-inch high-velocity bullet.[7] In the film, they appear to fall over like miniature Buster Keatons.

---

5 A steep, natural depression in the ground 80 yards in front of the Sunken Lane.

6 Believed to be the first men in history filmed being killed in action.

7 The rounds were probably from the machine guns on the Beaucourt Ridge (map references Q5d79.69 and Q6c10.70 in Panorama ❹) or the Bergwerk (in Panorama ❸), which caused the 16th Middlesex terrible casualties on the ground approaching the crater.

Fold out for Panorama ❹: *Hawthorn Ridge*

From his position behind the Sunken Lane, Major Archibald Utterson, commander of the 29th Division's reserve, observed the slaughter of the Fusiliers and Middlesex soldiers. At 9.45 a.m., he gathered together thirty of his remaining able-bodied men. Fully aware that they were going forward only to draw fire to themselves, they made a dash to the Sunken Lane. Only Utterson and four others made it. In front of Beaumont Hamel, it was the last 'offensive' manoeuvre of the day.

By 10.00 a.m., there was calm. For a time, firing on both sides ceased altogether. British bodies and German machine guns were allowed to cool. The surviving British soldiers were given their rations. The whole-bodied dead – or at least those within close reach of the British positions – were placed in tidy rows and their identity discs collected.

A further attack was planned for 12.30 p.m., but Colonel Magniac, commander of the 1st Lancs, reported that his total force in the front line and Sunken Lane now amounted to 125 effective soldiers, two officers and himself. The attack was called off. Fenced in by new lines of wire erected by Royal Engineers during the afternoon, a party of 25 men remained in the Sunken Lane overnight. Corporal Ashurst was one of them. The next morning he saw three oblivious Germans walking amongst the landfill of khaki bodies. He shot one of them.[8] A retaliating German barrage forced the Sunken Lane to be evacuated.

Malins and MacDowell's footage was edited into a 77-minute feature, *The Battle of the Somme*, which had its première in London on 10 August and was released generally on the 21st. In six weeks it was watched by 20 million people.[9] The scenes were sanitised, of course, yet they still showed filth, exhaustion, shellfire, the wounded, killing and the dead.[10] The audience was shocked, but they felt it was time that they were.

Today it is not the 'horror' that disturbs us, but the soldiers as they look at us through the camera. The ones that smile shame us with their cheerfulness. Those that don't offer a silent rebuke: 'This is what we did,' they say.

* * *

The Lynchet is now the site of Beaumont Hamel British Cemetery, the grass path to which can be seen in Panorama ❸: in it, 111 British soldiers, one Canadian and one Newfoundlander are buried. Most of the British are Lancashire Fusiliers from 1 July. The wooded darkness of the Hawthorn Mine crater can be reached by a path from the Beaumont Road. It is a discernibly unhappy place. Fragments of bone are still found on the surface.

The cemetery on the right of Panorama ❹ is Hawthorn Ridge No. 1 Cemetery, in which 152 British soldiers and one Newfoundlander are buried. Again, most of them were killed on 1 July. They were recovered from the ground in front of the crater by a V Corps burial detail in the spring of 1917.

---

8 The position from which Ashurst fired was precisely that from which Panorama ❸ was taken. The Germans were standing somewhere just this side of the three mature trees that line the fence to the right.

9 No other film until *Star Wars* commanded a comparable British audience.

10 Ironically the scene more obviously showing a British soldier fall in action (prompting a woman at the first night to stand up and scream, 'He's dead!') had been staged for the cameras some way behind the lines. The authentic frames went completely unnoticed.

RT-SUR-ANCRE
2900 yds

Station Road
M.G.s
1280 yds

M.G.
Q10b99.27 460yds

M.G.
Q11c 55.68 830 yds

St. Pierre Divion Church
3000 yds

Y-Ravine
Enemy Front Line
420 yds

M.G
Q17a82.77 1200yds

A M E L

I D G E

of Church
60,93 840yds

Beaucourt Road
1600 yds

Enemy Front Line
420yds

Station Alley
1650 yds

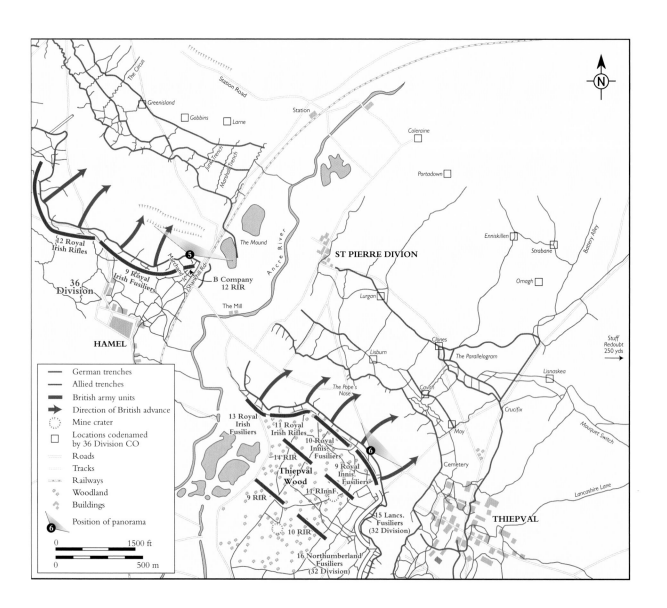

N

The Circus

Station Road

Greenisland

Gobbins

Larne

Station

Coleraine

Portadown

Junk Trench

Marshall Trench

The Mound

Enniskillen

Strabane

Ancre River

Omagh

12 Royal
Irish Rifles

St Pierre Divion

Marching St.

5

Shankhill Rd.

9 Royal
Irish Fusiliers

B Company
12 RIR

Lurgan

36
Division

The Mill

Clones

Stuff
Redoubt
250 yds

HAMEL

Lisburn

The Parallelogram

Lisnaskea

The Pope's
Nose

Cavan

Crucifix

13 Royal
Irish
Fusiliers

11 Royal
Irish Rifles

10 Royal
Innis.
Fusiliers

6

Moy

Mouquet Switch

14 RIR

9 Royal
Innis.
Fusiliers

Cemetery

Thiepval
Wood

11 RInnF.

Lancashire Lane

9 RIR

THIEPVAL

10 RIR

15 Lancs.
Fusiliers
(32 Division)

16 Northumberland
Fusiliers
(32 Division)

German trenches

Allied trenches

British army units

Direction of British advance

Mine crater

Locations codenamed
by 36 Division CO

Roads

Tracks

Railways

Woodland

Buildings

6   Position of panorama

0   1500 ft

0   500 m

CHAPTER 4

THE ANCRE VALLEY & THE SCHWABEN REDOUBT

As early as January 1914, newspapers across Britain were forecasting imminent war. This war was expected to be vicious and bloody. The British army would face a disciplined and growing force under able and determined leadership. Volunteer soldiers were already being drilled in readiness, women and children were being evacuated, and stocks of food and ammunition had been prepared. A Royal Navy squadron was already cruising the enemy coast. Yet this war was expected not across the English Channel but across the Irish Sea.

Since Prime Minister Herbert Asquith's introduction of the third Home Rule Bill in 1912, tensions had risen sharply across the Irish political divide. In January 1913, 80,000 Ulstermen under the Unionist leader Sir Edward Carson formed the Ulster Volunteer Force, resolving to resist home rule by force of arms if necessary. The nationalists responded in November by forming the Irish Volunteers. Both sides smuggled in guns and ammunition from Germany in preparation for civil war. The British government seemed powerless to stem the crisis.

When it ordered troops into Ulster to protect arms depots in March 1914, 57 out of the 70 British officers at the army's headquarters at Curragh resigned. By early summer, a bloodbath in Ireland seemed close at hand – but another war was to intervene.

On 5 July 1914, the German kaiser received Count Ladislaus Szogyeny, the 73-year-old Austro-Hungarian ambassador, at the Neues Palais in Potsdam. Over lunch, the kaiser confirmed Germany's support for Emperor Franz Josef's ultimatum to Serbia.[1] It was this ultimatum that Sir Edward Grey, the British Foreign Secretary, quietly read out to the British cabinet on 24 July. The First Lord of the Admiralty, Winston Churchill, was present. 'The parishes of Fermanagh and Tyrone faded back into the mists and squalls of Ireland,' he wrote later, 'and a strange light began immediately, but by perceptible gradations, to fall and grow upon the map of Europe.' It was no longer the Ulstermen's destiny to fight British soldiers on the banks of the Lagan; instead they would fight Germans in France.[2]

---

1 The kaiser's so-called 'blank cheque' to Austria Hungary. Some have speculated that the threat of civil war within the United Kingdom encouraged him to make it considerably blanker than it otherwise might have been.

2 Out of a total of 116,972 Irishmen (excluding officers) who volunteered for the British army between August 1914 and January 1918, 64,607 were Catholic. Enlisting for adventure, out of poverty or in response to Irish Party leader John Redmond's proclamation that 'The interests of Ireland – of the whole of Ireland – are at stake in this war,' they signed the oath of loyalty (though many deliberately misspelt their names) to the king. When the survivors returned, the political atmosphere had changed. Redmond's Irish Party won only 6 of 105 seats in the 1918 election. The militant nationalism of Éamon de Valera's Sinn Fein was in the ascendancy. In post-independence Ireland, the Catholic Irishmen who had fought in British uniform were officially forgotten. It was not until 1988 that the Irish National War Memorial Gardens, 5 km from parliament on the outskirts of Dublin, were formally dedicated and opened to the public.

M. G.
Q 176 24.19   750 yds

B E A U M O N T   H A M E
2300 yds

British Front Line
Hawthorn Ridge
2300 yds

M. G.
Q 176 63. 40 750 yds

The Circus
1050 yds

Like most of Lord Kitchener's volunteers, the 36th Ulster Division was to see its first major action at the Somme on 1 July 1916. Eight of its battalions would lead the attack along the River Ancre, a small tributary of the Somme running south through the British sector. On the left bank, the 12th Royal Irish Rifles and 9th Royal Irish Fusiliers would advance along the railway line towards Beaucourt. On the right, the 13th Royal Irish Fusiliers, the 11th Royal Irish Rifles and two Royal Inniskilling battalions would advance between St Pierre Divion and Thiepval. Facing the Ulstermen to the west of the marshes in the river valley was a ravine, in places 30 feet deep. In front of those on the rising ground to the east lay the subterranean German fortress of the Schwaben Redoubt.[3]

When the German advance had ground to a halt in October 1914, the invaders were free to choose where to mount their defences. On the heights north of the Somme, they chose better than anywhere else on the Western Front. Whilst the high water table of Flanders invariably swamped dugouts, German engineers could dig as deep as they liked in the Picardy chalk. Over the final months of 1914, they sculpted labyrinthine systems of earthworks as complex as small towns. The Thiepval ridge was like an anthill, with the Schwaben the nest of the queen. The geometric substructure housed a hospital, a telephone exchange and more than 1,000 men at a depth of 30 feet. The relentless British bombardment before the attack did little more in the Schwaben than force a flicker from the newly installed electric lights.

For every division other than the 36th, the two-day postponement of the attack due to heavy rain meant two more days of trembling anticipation. But for the Ulstermen assembling in Hamel and Thiepval Wood, it could not have seemed more auspicious. On the same date for which the advance was now scheduled, their forebears had defeated the Jacobites on the Boyne and assured Protestant ascendancy in Ireland. Now, 226 years later, albeit against a mostly Protestant German army, Carson's men would march to victory too.

In the trenches flanking the Ancre, men kissed family photographs and knelt silently and prayed. Hymns were sung and communion was taken. At 6.45 a.m., men of the 14th Royal Irish Rifles witnessed an all too human bodily sacrifice of their own. A party of bombers in Thiepval Wood was making final preparations in a closely packed trench when a box of grenades was knocked to the ground by a shell blast, dislodging the pins from two of them. Without hesitation, a 20-year-old linen apprentice from Belfast, William McFadzean, dived onto the grenades before they exploded. Despite the air being alive with shrapnel, men removed their helmets as his remains were removed on a stretcher. McFadzean was posthumously awarded the Victoria Cross.[4]

For some, the strain of the morning proved too much. One Ulsterman resorted to his water bottle that he had filled with wine, and drank himself insensible. *Hors de combat* at zero hour, he is reputed to

---

3 It was known to the 36th Division, on account of its shape, as 'The Parallelogram'.

4 The Victoria Cross awarded to 'Billy' McFadzean (pronounced 'McFadjun') was presented to his father at Buckingham Palace on 28 February 1917; he was given a return train ticket for the journey, 3rd class. Out of the nine VCs awarded (six posthumously) for actions on 1 July, four were received by Ulstermen.

Fold out for Panorama ❺: *The Ancre Valley*

have woken 'fighting mad' in the early afternoon and charged into no man's land. He was later taken prisoner by the Germans.

At 7.30 a.m., the Ulsters advanced at the signal of a bugle. Such was their fervour, the Derrys and Tyrones were already yards from the German lines before it had sounded. They all knew their destinations well. The division commander, Major-General Oliver Nugent, had codenamed key locations on the battlefield using placenames from the Irish North. Some men wore their Orange Order sashes over their bulky equipment. As well as a soldier's own 60 pounds of kit, additional equipment could include trench ladders, duckboards, pickets, Bangalore torpedoes, flares, semaphore flags, telephone wire, telephones, mortars, Lewis and Vickers machine guns and ammunition. Some men looked less like an assaulting army than people moving house. Lieutenant-Colonel Ambrose Ricardo, the Tyrones' commanding officer, stood on the parapet and watched them file through the exits into no man's land. 'They got through without delay; no fuss, no shouting, no running, everything solid and thorough – just like the men themselves. Here and there a boy would wave his hand to me as I shouted a good luck to them through my megaphone. And all had a cheery face. Most were carrying heavy loads. Fancy advancing against heavy fire with a big roll of barbed wire on your shoulder!'

The first men to advance towards the Schwaben, however, did so at the double, some older hands having ditched their packs. With shells still falling, and lent at least visual cover from tall grasses, the four lead battalions won the race to the parapet of the German front lines around *Lurgan*, *Lisburn* and *Cavan*. The Germans were slow to scale the steps of their shelters. They had a lot of steps to climb. As they emerged, the Riflemen 'potted them like ferreted rabbits'. 'Hun got tired of this and the survivors surrendered.' More than 500 prisoners were taken. Sixteen at a time were escorted at the prod of a single bayonet back to the British lines. One British soldier was seen escorting back more than 60 surrendering Germans, 'holding them together as jealously as a sheepdog holds his flock, urging along the laggards, keeping ever behind the last man of his party'. In an effort to dodge the effects of their own barrage, some prisoners sprinted towards the British lines and were bayoneted by supporting waves of Irishmen leaving Thiepval Wood. At 7.47 a.m., a message from the 9th Inniskillings was received by telephone at their battalion HQ: 'All is well,' the voice said.

On the other side of the river, the signs were not so propitious. The men from Antrim, Armagh, Cavan and Monaghan had moved up to their own wire ten minutes before zero hour, leaving behind their '10 per cent'.[5] Even though a smokescreen obscured their advance, the German artillery batteries and machine-gunners had their target lines pre-set to a yard and they fired into the smoke. On the left, only a Sergeant Hamilton and four other soldiers from the 12th Irish Rifles reached the German front line. Most didn't make the ravine. By 8.30 a.m., news that their attack had broken was sent back by runner. The runner returned with orders for the remaining men to retire to the British lines.

5 By this stage in the war, it was standard procedure for a battalion to leave 10 per cent of its strength (and a much greater proportion of officers and NCOs) in reserve during an attack. In the event of annihilating casualties, these men would form the basis of a new unit. Subalterns of the 9th RIF drew lots to determine who would go and who would stay. Those who 'won' joined in the attack. Those who 'lost' went on a transport course in Le Havre.

made at *c.7.30 am BST* on *1st July 2015* from *Marchand St/Shankill Road : 9th Royal Irish Fusiliers 7.30am BST 1st July 1916*
including a field view of *154°* from about *WNW* to *ESE*

Approximate Scale of Degrees (1 degree equals *1/3* inches).

| 2 | 3 | 4 | 5 | 6 | 7 | 8 | 9 | 10 | 11 | 12 |

St PIERRE DIVION
1050 yds

Portadown
R13d.7.9 1740 yds

Enniskillen
R14c.1.2 1490 yds

The Mound
490 yds

BEAUCOURT-SUR-ANCRE
2100 yds

M.G.
Q18e 61.41 360 yds

M.G.
Q18c 55.78 500 yds

M.G.
Q18a 95.45
850 yds

Ancre River
750 yds

Coleraine
R13 b 3.4 1850 yds

FC

Pa

0

On the right, as the smoke cleared, the subsequent waves of the 9th Royal Irish Fusiliers were observed in a mirror by the crew of German machine gun no.7 (map reference Q18c61.41 on Panorama ❺). Scores of Fusiliers were dismembered at close range. With cries of 'Faugh a Ballagh' (a regimental Irish battle cry, literally translated as 'clear the way'), a handful of Ulstermen managed to penetrate the German lines near *The Circus*, and nine men from the 12th Royal Irish Rifles under a Lieutenant Lemon (attacking on the right flank of the 9th RIF towards Beaucourt station) got as far as the German second line. Only a Rifleman McNeilly from this party reported for roll call at the close of the day. The few other men on the north side of the ravine now came under fire from the machine guns just north of Station Road, as well as from Erdmörsers, particularly vicious over-sized canister shells filled with high explosive and scrap metal. They clung on in shell holes, but would advance no further. At 9.00 a.m., German signallers of Reserve Infanterie Regiment 119 reported that the attack on this sector was over.

Across the river, east of St Pierre Divion, soldiers of the 11th Royal Irish Rifles had consolidated a position at *Clones*. Together with men from the 9th and 10th 'Skins', they now pressed up to the Schwaben from three sides. In a 'Belfast riot on top of Mount Vesuvius', the Ulstermen fought a vicious 'streetfight' with grenades, trench knives and rifle butts. For almost all, it was their first experience of bayoneting, an experience described by one as akin to thrusting 'a knifepoint into chilled butter'. One Inniskilling had improvised his own weapon from a pick shaft and a pear-shaped lump of cast-iron. 'No matter where it hit a man it broke bones,' a fellow 'Skin' later wrote. 'He must have killed a dozen Germans. The blood had got about the tongue of our boots and our socks were soaked with it.' German

and British wounded lay together in the maze of trenches. 'I found a German, badly wounded,' recorded a Lance Corporal J. A. Henderson of the Belfast Young Citizens. 'I could see from his face that he was mad with thirst. I gave him my water, although it was against orders. Then I found one of our men; he was terribly wounded, shot in the head and his leg nearly off. He begged me to kill him, but I couldn't do it.'

Behind the leading Ulster battalions, the follow-up 107th Brigade now left Thiepval Wood. To their right, the attack of the 32nd Division in front of Thiepval had collapsed. Five German machine guns in the village were now turned west towards the Ulsters. Division HQ had issued orders that no battalion staff should join their men, but with their soldiers beginning to fall in large numbers, Lieutenant-Colonel F. P. Crozier and Lieutenant-Colonel H.C. Bernard, the COs of the 9th and 10th RIRs, now disobeyed. A trench mortar barrage from Thiepval killed Bernard as he left the wood, and also destroyed his two leading companies following behind in columns of four. Rallying the remainder between puffs on a Woodbine, the portly Crozier flung himself across the sunken road followed by his breathless batman. Major George Gaffikin echoed his call with the Boyne battle cry. Taking off the orange sash of his order and holding it above his head, he shouted 'No surrender!' Losing one in every three men to machine-gun bullets, the Ulstermen pushed forward as if into a heavy blizzard. Passing through *Moy*, they joined the battle for the Schwaben. By 8.45, it was in British hands. By mid-morning, groups of Royal Irish Riflemen had reached the Pozières Ridge.

If the Ulstermen were not surprised by the extent of their advance, the Germans were. Unteroffizier Felix Kircher was one of the few soldiers in *Stuff Redoubt*: 'Suddenly, an observer shouted down the dugout steps in amazement, "Tommy is here, come up!" We rushed up and saw a lot of khaki-clothed men. Most of them were just boys like us – about twenty years old. We were in a desperate situation. We had no weapons or ammunition. We were purely artillery observers.' Relief for Kircher came not from German reinforcements but from British artillery. With the battlefield shrouded in smoke, and communication now reduced to hand-delivered messages, the batteries could not easily adjust their ranges to keep pace with events.[6] Most frequently on 1 July, timetabled British barrages fell long, but here, due to the extent of the Ulsters' advance, the shells fell fatally short. The leading British men were forced to fall back. 'If the English could have got through,' Kircher added, 'they would have only met clerks, cooks and orderlies.' It was the decisive moment in the battle.

On learning of the breach to the German lines, an impatient Generalmajor von Soden of 26 Reserve Infanterie Division immediately ordered that the defending Württembergers be reinforced. Further troops arrived by train at Grandcourt station at 2.03 p.m. An additional 10,000 hand grenades were brought up to the regimental sector. The isolated British soldiers in *Lisnaskea*, *Omagh* and *Strabane* were now counter-attacked from the north and east. The Germans took a number of prisoners, many of whom were wounded, including Captain Charles Craig, the extremely large Unionist MP for South Antrim. He was escorted to the German lines in a wheelbarrow.

The Irishmen retreated to the Schwaben Redoubt, now the main British line of defence, although with Thiepval uncaptured there was little hope of holding on to it. Throughout the afternoon, German bombing teams trailed the Ulstermen through their network of familiar trenches, the sticks on their grenades giving them an advantage in throwing distance. With visibility extending only as far as the next traverse, fighting was tense and brutal. The British moved inexorably backwards.

One of von Soden's most seasoned veterans, Unteroffizier Friedrich Hinkel, and his small group of Westphalians had held a trench to the south of the Schwaben since dawn. His best shot, a farm boy known as the 'Stammler' (stammerer), had personally accounted for over twenty Ulstermen. They now witnessed the reversal of the battle: 'The British retreated in droves from the Schwaben Reboubt. Once again, our machine guns rattled away. Once again, our rifles glowed red hot. Once again my men were seized with the reckless bravado that had gripped them that morning. Many an Irish mother's son lay down to the eternal sleep from which there is no awakening.'

The dwindling ranks of Ulstermen fought grimly on – one cornering a hunting party of Germans in a dugout and burning them to death with a Bangalore torpedo – but after ten intense hours they were short of energy, fluids and, increasingly, resolve. It has been said by soldiers that courage is a finite reserve drawn on in combat. By early

---

6 Communication at battalion headquarters was further complicated by the intermittent arrival of messages that had nothing to do with the fighting. In the middle of the battle, Captain N. Strong of the Derry Volunteers received a message from a brigade staff officer. Delivered by two runners, one of whom had been hit on the way, it read: 'Please re-submit drawing of the foot of Pte. Warke, size of boot 13.' (An inspection of the Forces War Records confirms that 26-year-old Private Joseph Warke from Donegal, of the 10th Inniskillings, was killed in action on 1 July.) Another unknown staff officer also issued the following order that day to the fighting units of III and VIII Corps: 'Certain complaints have been received that no pork can be found in the tins … Troops must not be misled by the name pork and beans, and expect to find a full ration of pork; as a matter of fact the pork is practically all absorbed by the beans.'

Panorama No. *6* made at *c.7.30 am BST* on *1st July 2015* from *the end of George St: 9th Royal Inniskilling Fusiliers 730am BST 1st*

including a field view of *135°* from about *NNW* to *SE*

Approximate Scale of Degrees (1 degree equals *1/3* inches).

0   1   2   3   4   5   6   7   8   9   10

St PIERRE DIVION
1050 yds

The Pope's Nose
R19c2.5   400 yds
M.G.

The Mill
R13a25.68 1700 yds

Lisburn
R19c3.7 500yds

Lurgan
R19a4.4 900yds

Coleraine
R18b3.4 1970yds

Enemy F.
390

M.G.
R19c42.41 540yds

evening, the reserves of some Ulstermen had run out. 'A strong rabble of tired, hungry and thirsty stragglers approach me from the east,' wrote Lieutenant-Colonel F. P. Crozier later in his 1930 memoir, *A Brass Hat in No Man's Land*. 'I go out to meet them. "Where are you going?" I ask. One says one thing, one another. They are marched to the water reserve, given a drink and hunted back to the fight. Another more formidable party cuts across to the south. They mean business. They are damned if they are going to stay, it's all up. A young sprinting subaltern heads them off. They push by him. He draws his revolver and threatens them. They take no notice. He fires. Down drops a British soldier at his feet. The effect is instantaneous. They turn back to their comrades in distress.'

By 6.00 p.m., fewer than 300 men remained inside the Redoubt. Major Peacocke of the 9th Inniskillings sent a message to the rear: 'Please do all that you can to send up Vickers machine gun belts, bombs and SAA [small arms ammunition]. I think we shall hold on only men are rather done up.' An hour later, a further message was received from Lieutenant McClure of the 10th Skins just south of the Crucifix, the gist of which was the same. Only 120 men remained. Short of water and ammunition, they were described as 'rather done up' too.

At 10.00 p.m., Peacocke ordered all remaining men to withdraw to the German front line. The wounded were left to cope as best they could. 'We collected all the ammunition we could from our own dead, a terrible task, but it was necessary,' one Ulsterman recalled, 'for we knew we would need every bullet we could get. In the big trench we set up sentries and some of us tried to get some rest. It was hard for we kept seeing the bits and pieces of the dead bodies and the terrible bleeding of the wounded, and the smell of the sweat and the hunger kept us from sleeping.' By

midnight, every able-bodied Ulsterman was back where he had started.

Nearly 10,000 volunteer soldiers of the 36th Division had gone into battle during sixteen hours of fighting. Men in their ranks had advanced further into enemy territory than any other unit on the whole 15-mile front that day. Yet by the end of it they had given up their gains, and 5,500 of them had become casualties.

Major-General Nugent wrote to his wife the next day: 'The Ulster Division has been too superb for words. The whole army is talking of the incomparable gallantry shown by officers and men. They went forward with every line dressed as if for the King's inspection, torn from end to end by shell and machine gun fire. The Ulster Division no longer exists as a fighting force. It has proved itself and it has indeed borne itself like men. I cannot describe to you how I feel about them. I did not believe men were made who could do such gallant work under the conditions of modern war.'

'We were never prouder of our province and our race than we are at this moment,' the *Northern Whig* newspaper declared as the scale of the losses became clear at home, 'for it means more today than it ever did to be an Ulsterman.' The Most Reverend Dr John Baptist Crozier, Archbishop of Armagh and Primate of all Ireland, agreed, writing in the *Belfast News-Letter* that he 'expected nothing else. They are of the stock from which our heroes come and to whom our Empire owes so much – unconquered and unconquerable.' The ultimate accolade came shortly after the Armistice from the King Emperor in whose name they had fought: 'In these days of rejoicing I recall the deeds of the 36th Division … Throughout the long years of struggle which have now so gloriously ended, the men of Ulster have proved how nobly they fight and die.'

Two months earlier, the Easter Rising had added a new list of sacrificial heroes to the cause of Irish Nationalism. The nascent province of a Unionist Northern Ireland now had its martyrs too.

* * *

In Panorama ❺, the cemetery located in the ravine over which the Ulstermen crossed is Ancre British Cemetery, where 2,500 British soldiers are buried or commemorated: over half of them are unidentified.

In Panorama ❻, the cemetery in which the photograph is taken is Connaught Cemetery, where 1,268 British soldiers are buried, at least half of whom are Irishmen killed on 1 July. Of the 643 unknown soldiers here, 482 could not even be identified to their unit.

The cemetery on the horizon is Mill Road Cemetery, holding 1,304 British soldiers (mostly Ulstermen), and built on the site of the Schwaben Redoubt. The ground here continues to shift and subside, and unusually the gravestones are therefore laid flat.

The Ulster Tower (on the left) is Northern Ireland's National War Memorial. One of the first memorials to be erected on the Western Front (it was opened on 19 November 1921), it commemorates the men of the 36th (Ulster) Division) and all those from Ulster who served in the Great War. It is modelled on **Helen's Tower** in the grounds of the **Clandeboye Estate**, near Bangor, County Down, where many of the men of the Ulster Division trained before leaving for France.

1. Panoramas are taken solely for military purposes.
2. The publication of them in the press will necessarily give valuable information to the enemy.
3. This panorama is to be kept with as much security as is compatible with full advantage of it being taken by our own troops.
4. When troops are relieved this panorama should be handed over to the relieving troops.

THIEPVAL

Lancashire Lane
1120 yds

Mouquet Farm
R 336 28.95 2600 yds

Enemy Front Line
460 yds

M.G
R 256 31.74 560 yds

M.G
R 256 22.22 540 yds

Cemetery
R 256 7.6 690 yds

M.G.
R19d23.20
500yds

Crucifix
R19d89.28 850yds

Stuff Redoubt
2100yds

Lisnaskea
R20c7.3 1220yds

Moy
R2563.9 480yds

M.G
R20c39.39 1080yds

M.G
R20c24 1025yds

Mouquet Switch
1330 yds

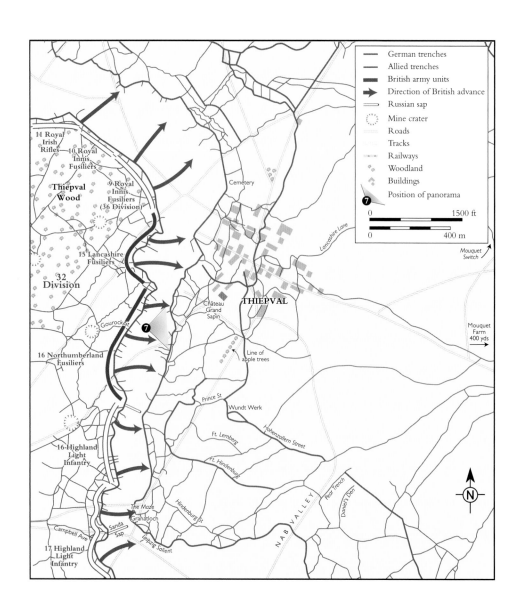

German trenches
Allied trenches
British army units
Direction of British advance
Russian sap
Mine crater
Roads
Tracks
Railways
Woodland
Buildings
❼ Position of panorama

0   1500 ft
0   400 m

11 Royal
Irish
Rifles
10 Royal
Innis.
Fusiliers
9 Royal
Innis.
Fusiliers
(36 Division)

Thiepval
Wood

Cemetery

15 Lancashire
Fusiliers

32
Division

Gourock St

Château
Grand
Sapin

THIEPVAL

Lancashire Lane

Mouquet
Switch

Mouquet
Farm
400 yds

❼

16 Northumberland
Fusiliers

Line of
apple trees

Prince St
Wundt Werk
Ft. Lemberg
Ft. Hindenburg

Hohenzollern Street

16 Highland
Light
Infantry

The Maze
Grahatloch
Campbell Ave
Sanda
Sap
Leipzig Salient

Hindenburg St

N A B V A L L E Y

Pear Trench

Daniel's Den

17 Highland
Light
Infantry

N

CHAPTER 5

THIEPVAL

When Sir Edwin Lutyens was charged after the war with designing a memorial to the missing of the Somme, he was in no doubt where it should be built. The Thiepval plateau is less than 500 feet above sea level, yet it still dominates the whole of the Ancre Valley. From here, Lutyens's great ziggurat-like structure of dry blood-coloured brick and white stone presides over almost every view from the northern battlefield. The Germans too had seen the significance of this great shoulder of chalk as a vital natural buttress to the flatter land east to Bapaume. In the autumn of 1914 they had occupied the village of Thiepval without a fight. There they decided to stay. If they hadn't, Lutyens's memorial might not have been inscribed with so many names.

When the Germans arrived, Thiepval was a semi-feudal community of 93 houses, 200 people and a new church.[1] For the younger inhabitants of the village, the German occupation was an unwelcome novelty, but for those old enough to remember the Franco-Prussian War of 1870, it was ruefully familiar. Many residents had already fled west to the safety of Amiens, the new squire of Thiepval amongst them. A retired Parisian engineer, Henri Portier had bought the elegant 1725 Château Grand Sapin from the childless Comte de Breda two years earlier, a transaction that marked the end of local seigneurial rule and one of the worst property deals in history. The old palace on the hill now stood empty, its 94 windows crudely boarded against the vistas to come. M. Portier's residency had lasted six weeks.

The fighting here on 1 July was shortlived. Histories of the day's fighting invariably spare it only a few paragraphs. There are also few first-hand accounts – not many British soldiers survived to write them. And few that did felt inclined to tell the tale of two thousand north-country Englishmen walking slowly up a hill to get shot.

The battle is notable for the bland assurances of British commanding officers before the attack. One brigadier-general told the Newcastles: 'You will be able to go over with a walking stick; you will not need rifles. When you get to Thiepval you will find the Germans all dead. Not even a rat will have survived.' Major-General W. H. Rycroft, commanding officer of the 32nd Division, promised his men that they would find nothing but 'the caretaker and his dog'. Their confidence stemmed in no small part from the assignment by X Corps HQ of two 9.2-inch howitzers to destroy the bunkers and cellars beneath the village. In the event, a shellburst in one gun

---

1 The old one had burned down during the Franco-Prussian War (1870–71).

'd

1. Panoramas are taken solely for military purposes.
2. The publication of them in the press will necessarily give valuable information to the enemy.
3. This panorama is to be kept with as much security as is compatible with full advantage of it being taken by
   our own troops.

1916 4. When troops are relieved this panorama should be handed over to the relieving troops.

12

Lancashire Lane
1250 yds

T H I E P V A L

Enemy Front Line
150 yds

FOURTH ARMY.

Map

Panorama No. **7** made at **7.30 am. BST** on c. *1st July 2015* from *Gourock St/ Hamilton Ave: 16th Northumberland Fusilie*

including a field view of **94°** from about **NE** to **SE**

Approximate Scale of Degrees (1 degree equals **½** inches).

0   1   2   3   4   5   6   7   8   9   10

Mouquet Swit
1650 yds

Stuff Redoubt
21c4.9 2450 yds

M.G
R25b 22.22. 710 yds

Château Gra
R25d 25.50 4.

M.G.
R25c 78.58 330 yds

Enemy Front Line
220 yds

M.G.
R25c 76.45 300 yds

put both out of action. Lighter shells proved useless. The seven-day British bombardment failed to destroy any of the garrison's machine guns and injured only three men from their crews.[2]

Soldiers' wills (all soldiers' pay books had a page given over to the purpose) and final notes to mothers and wives were not the only words hastily scribbled during the last few hours' waiting. There were autographs too. Two Newcastle United footballers were in the ranks of the 16th Northumberland Fusiliers: Corporal Dan Dunglinson had played at St James's Park as an amateur full back before the war, and Private Tommy Goodwill, an ex-coalminer, had joined United for £100 in May 1913. A gifted outside left, known as the 'darling of the Leazes End', Goodwill played 60 first-team games for Newcastle, with his last before enlisting being a 3–0 home win over Aston Villa on 28 April 1915. Lord Kitchener had appealed particularly to the nation's professional soccer stars to join the colours. Of the 40 players on Newcastle's books, 27 stepped forward. On the morning of 1 July, Goodwill and Dunglinson were given a ball and put in the first wave of the attack.

The Newcastle men would attack to the right of the now-ruined chateau. The Salford Pals on their left would assault the village head-on up a hill. Almost every battalion that advanced that morning would do so up some sort of gradient. The Salfords had the steepest ascent of all: in crossing the 300 yards to the German trenches, they would have to climb 80 feet.

Like all those detailed to lead the first waves, the young officers in the forward Salford and Newcastle trenches had inspected their luminous watches throughout the night. Now, at 7.29 a.m., it was the small subsidiary seconds dial, set in place of the '6', that most officers watched with their lips pursed around their whistles. The single, hair-thin black hand slowly ticked its way to the '60' mark. The shrill blasts of what sounded like a dozen indignant policemen signalled zero hour.

Much cheering greeted the whistles, and trench ladders were climbed at speed – or as much speed as was possible for soldiers carrying the equivalent weight of six adult-size ten-pin bowling balls. The first 200 men over the top of the two battalions' trenches then started to walk towards the enemy. Today many people assume that the image of British soldiers strolling haplessly into machine-gun fire is a myth. But, while some battalions in some sectors of the battlefield did employ looser formations and rush tactics, most of the advancing troops did in fact walk. They had been told to. It was the invariable class assumption of British commanders that civilian soldiers from the industrial heartlands of northern England were incapable of carrying out a more complicated instruction.

They were also told what pattern to walk in. Divisional headquarters issued battalion commanders with diagrams illustrating the disposition of their platoons. Inch-long bars filled in with coloured pencil

---

2   Over the seven days of the British preliminary bombardment, 1,070 field guns and 467 heavy guns manned by 50,000 gunners fired 1,508,652 shells on the German lines at a cost of £6 million. These figures appeared impressive, but the confidence they generated was illusory. Although more than four times as many heavy guns were deployed on the Somme as at the battle of Loos in 1915 (the biggest British offensive up to that date, and a bloody failure), the Somme battlefront was so long that the number of shells per square yard was increased by only about 125 per cent. The need to bombard three lines of German defences as opposed to a single front line reduced the density of the shelling even further. In any case, even the heavy guns (for which about a third of the shells were faulty) were insufficient to destroy bunkers as deep and strong as those the Germans had on the Somme. Only super-heavy howitzers were capable of doing the job, and the British had only six of them on the whole of the Somme battlefield.

Fold out for Panorama ⑦: *Thiepval*

denoted the assaulting waves. Arrows and the number of yards indicated the spaces between them. The first four waves would advance at intervals of 50 yards. (In a variation of doubtless devilish cunning, the second four would advance at intervals of 75 yards.) Most of the British generals had grown up in the 1860s and 1870s, when playing with early lead soldiers was all the rage. Tactical precedent, together with the fact that these expensive, hand-painted figures were invariably cast in only one pose, dictated that they were arranged in satisfying Napoleonic lines. The High Command chose to arrange their flesh-and-blood soldiers in just such lines on 1 July. In an effort to stick to the diagram, attacking soldiers frequently paused to 'dress' these lines – in other words, make sure they lined up. As a result, many of them were machine-gunned while looking sideways and shuffling backwards.

Whichever way they were looking, the first six waves of the 1st Salfords and 16th Northumberlands were annihilated. Corporal Dunglinson was one of the first men to be shot down.

'The British believed that it would just be a question of harvesting the fruits of their seven-day bombardment,' said the German report of the day. 'They were sorely deceived. Our shirtsleeved soldiers stood, knelt or lay flat as best enabled them to send a murderous massed fire into the continuous ranks of the British … who, directed by the little flags and sticks of their officers, were advancing in immaculate order. A wall of British dead was growing in front of our positions.'

Subsequent waves of British soldiers joined the procession into the intersecting arcs of at least nine German heavy machine guns, their gentle 'patter patter' at a distance belying their rapid rate of fire. The German machine-gunners favoured firing low. Bullets would shatter legs first, then deliver fatal wounds to the torso as the soldier collapsed. The plumes of earth rising in sequence from the ground or the cries of anguish from men to either side frequently made the moment when a soldier was hit predictable. Yet the men carried on walking. It was only when they found themselves on their own that they dropped to the ground and took whatever cover they could: many soldiers on 1 July were shot through their helmets. The Germans now abandoned cover themselves in their greed for blood. It was an enduring source of bitterness for the Geordie men that the defenders stood on their parapets to taunt them and wave them on.

The 16th Northumberlands' commanding officer, Colonel W. H. Ritson, had been one of the local Tyneside businessmen instrumental in raising the city's volunteer units. The 48-year-old had been with his battalion since their earliest days of training in the grounds of Newcastle Grammar School. Lance Corporal S. Henderson stood alongside him as he watched the carnage unfold: 'I vividly remember him standing in the British front line, tears streaming down his face, saying over and over, "My God! My boys! My boys!" I had to restrain him from going over himself. He would have been killed if he had.'

As Lieutenant-Colonel Crozier and his 9th Royal Irish Rifles moved up through Thiepval Wood to launch their supporting attack on the Schwaben Redoubt, he glanced to the right through a gap in the branches: 'I see the 10th Rifles plodding on and then my eyes are riveted on a sight I shall never see again. It is the 32nd Division at its best. I see rows upon rows of British soldiers lying dead, dying or wounded in no man's land.' Then, as he emerged from the trees: 'Again I look southward from a different angle and perceive heaped-up masses of British corpses

Hohenzollern Street
740 yds

Ft. Hindenburg
820 yds

N A B   V A L L E Y

WUNDT-WERK
R31 63.1 620yds
M.G s

Ft. Lemberg
620 yds

Enemy 2nd Line
340yds

M.G
R31a 83.83 240 yds

M.G.
R31a 69.78 170yds

M.G
R31a 69.78 170 yds

ont Line
yds

Enemy 3rd Line
550yds

Line of Apple Trees
R31632.85 470 yds
M.G

Mouquet Farm
R3363.8 2450 yds

POZIÈRE
3200 yds

Er

on the German wire in front of the Thiepval stronghold, while live men move forward in orderly procession to swell the weight of numbers in the spider's web. Will the last available and previously detailed man soon appear to do his futile duty unto death on the altar of sacrifice?'

In the mind of Lieutenant-General Morland, the X Corps commander, the answer strategically speaking was 'yes'. By 8.30 a.m., Morland had a reasonable grasp of how his troops had fared both to the left and in front of Thiepval. He therefore faced a choice of whether to reinforce the successful attack of the 109th Brigade (the Ulstermen) north of the Schwaben or to renew the failed assault of the 96th (the Salfords and Newcastles). So convinced was Major-General Perceval, commander of the 49th Division, that the full strength of his reserves should be thrown in to exploit the Ulstermen's gains that he personally visited the X Corps commander at his observation post two miles behind the lines. Perceval found Morland sitting up a tree, and climbed the steps to bring his opinion to bear. Morland conceded that one brigade could be moved up into Thiepval Wood, but otherwise the plan was unchanged. The 96th Brigade's attack would continue.

At 9.10 a.m., two companies from both the 2nd Salford Pals and the Newcastle Commercials advanced from the British trenches. Sketchy intelligence had suggested British troops had been seen in the village,[3] so the British batteries offered no artillery support. Captain Thomas F. Tweed from Eccles led B Company of the Salfords, most of whom he had personally enlisted, including Private Walter Fiddes, his orderly and a friend of his family. 'Through the perfect storm of

lead, the company went on,' Tweed wrote later. 'Ignoring the rain of death that whistled about them, they kept running from shell hole to shell hole, on and on. Pals of years' association dropped. Others fell, riddled with bullets, never to rise again. The cry was always "On, on."' B Company suffered 75 per cent casualties, their bodies adding to those already piled up on what was to become called the 'Bloody Road' – both a literal and a profane description – (now the D151 from Thiepval to Authuille). A month later, a piece appeared in a local Salford newspaper under the heading: 'THE ECCLES PALS. Message to Relatives from Capt. T. F. Tweed.' In it Tweed, who would go on to be a novelist and, from 1927 until his death in 1940, political adviser to Lloyd George, wrote: 'That I feel the loss of so many gallant men need not be stated. Most of my men I personally persuaded to join the colours and I felt the burden of responsibility for their welfare as a matter of both duty and honour, and now so many of them have made the supreme sacrifice, I wonder with what feelings their loved ones regard myself.'

The 180th Württemberger Regiment had held Thiepval since September 1914. By the evening of 1 July, they held it still, a record for any German unit on the Western Front. Over the following weeks, it became a point of honour for the garrison to retain the village at all costs. It took another bloody battle for British and Canadian troops to finally capture it on 25 September. In the aftermath of the Somme campaign, John Masefield described his visit to what remained of the place: 'It is as though the fight here had been more than to the death, to beyond

---

3 In fact, 100 men of the 1st Salfords had penetrated the German front line, but they were rapidly killed or forced to retreat.

death, to the bones and skeleton of the corpse which was yet unkillable … There is nothing left of the church; a long reddish mound of brick, that seems mainly powder round a core of cement, still marks where the chateau stood.'

On the first day of the long battle for the heights of Thiepval, over 700 Lancashire and Tyneside soldiers had died in less than two hours. Over a third of them, including Private Thomas Goodwill and Private Walter Fiddes, have no known grave. Their names are inscribed on the memorial whose great arch looms over the ground where they fell.

In 1933, for the second time in forty years, a small new red brick church was built in the village. It is dedicated to Our Lady of Peace.

* * *

Sir Edwin Lutyens's Memorial to the Missing of the Somme, at the centre of Panorama ❼, was inaugurated by the Prince of Wales in the presence of Albert Lebrun, President of France, on 1 August 1932.

Standing 140 ft high, it records the names of 72,195 British and South African soldiers killed on the Somme with no known grave. (The missing soldiers of other Commonwealth countries are commemorated elsewhere.) The Commonwealth War Graves Commission is committed to retaining the monument's integrity as a memorial to only the missing or unidentified of the battlefield. Over the last eighty years, therefore, the number of names inscribed on it has been reduced as men's bodies and identities have been discovered. Such men are re-buried in a cemetery near to where they died, and their names on the memorial are filled in with concrete. When this photograph was taken, the memorial was being refurbished in preparation for the centenary of the battle. The contractors just visible on the scaffolding give an idea of its size. When the foundations for the structure were excavated in May 1929, steps to three German dugouts were discovered, each still equipped with unexploded bombs and shells.

d

'916

12

L E I P Z I

G R A N

Turk Street
500 yds

Ft. Lemberg
370 yds

THE NAZE

Enemy Front Line
190 yds

Cabbage Street
290 yds

Mouquet Farm
R 33.6.3.8 2450 yds

Ft. Hinden
400 yds

Panorama No. **8** made at c.7.30 am BST on c.1st July 2015 from **N** of *Campbell Avenue:17th Highland Light Infantry* 7.30 am BS

including a field view of **99°** from about **NE** to **SE**

Approximate Scale of Degrees (1 degree equals **1/2** inches).

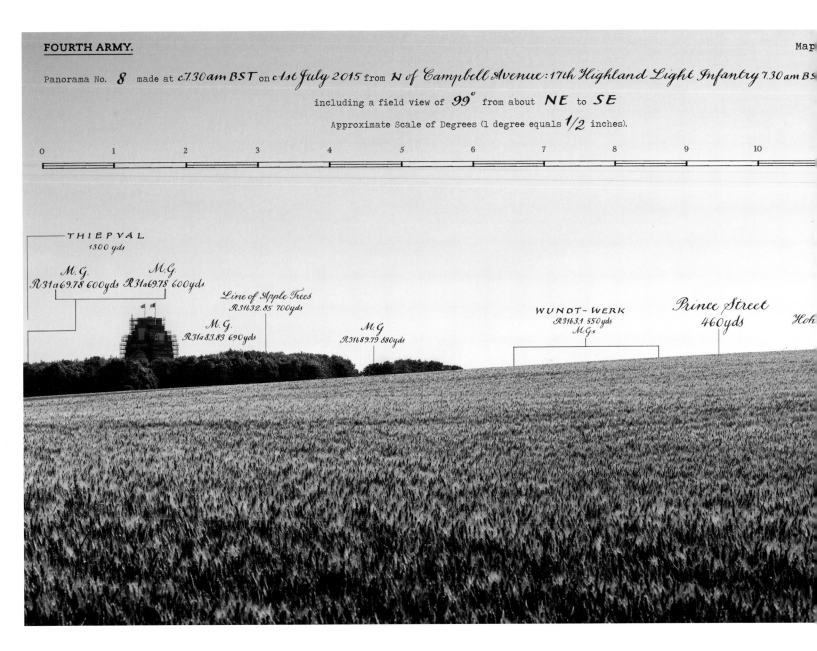

THIEPVAL
1300 yds

M.G.
R31a69.78 600yds

M.G.
R31a69.78 600yds

Line of Apple Trees
R31t32.85 700yds

M.G.
R31a83.83 690yds

M.G
R31t89.79 880yds

WUNDT-WERK
R31t3.1 550yds
M.Gs

Prince Street
460yds

Hoh

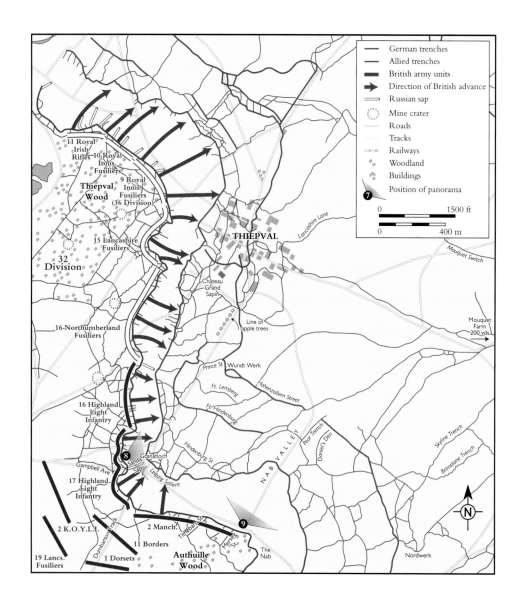

Legend:
- German trenches
- Allied trenches
- British army units
- Direction of British advance
- Russian sap
- Mine crater
- Roads
- Tracks
- Railways
- Woodland
- Buildings
- ⑦ Position of panorama

0 ___ 1500 ft

0 ___ 400 m

11 Royal Irish Rifles

10 Royal Innis. Fusiliers

9 Royal Innis. Fusiliers (36 Division)

Thiepval Wood

15 Lancashire Fusiliers

32 Division

16 Northumberland Fusiliers

16 Highland Light Infantry

⑧

17 Highland Light Infantry

2 K.O.Y.L.I.

19 Lancs. Fusiliers

1 Dorsets

11 Borders

2 Manch.

Authuille Wood

⑨

THIEPVAL

Lancashire Lane

Mouquet Switch

Château Grand Sapin

Line of apple trees

Mouquet Farm 200 yds

Prince St

Wundt Werk

Ft. Lemberg

Hohenzollern Street

Ft. Hindenburg

Hindenburg St.

Campbell Ave

Sanda Sap

Granatloch

Leipzig Salient

Dumbarton Track

Tithebarn St.

Mersey St.

The Nab

NAB VALLEY

Pear Trench

Daniel's Den

Skyline Trench

Brimstone Trench

Nordwerk

N

CHAPTER 6

THE LEIPZIG SALIENT & NAB VALLEY

In the early morning of 27 September 1914, a 52-year-old Frenchman set out from his farmhouse and waved goodbye to his wife. He lived in Authuille, a small village a mile down the 'Bloody Road' from Thiepval, earning his family's living from chickens, cows and an assortment of root crops. His name was Boromée Vaquette.

It was no distance from his smallholding on the edge of the village to the crest of the hill, and he knew the route well, a steady climb to fresh pasture and one of the finest views in northern France. Looking along the valley from Aveluy in the south to Miraumont on its northern curve, the scene had altered little since the early eighteenth century. Napoleon's introduction of sugar beet had been the only change to the ground in two hundred years. Royal woodlands of oak and sycamore still stood in thick belts, breaking up the hard-worked fields that rose and fell between the chalk lanes and villages.

As Vaquette goaded his six cows eastwards, the German army was heading west. It was 55 days since a nation at the forefront of Western progress had risked it all and invaded Belgium. Five weeks later, by 6 September, General von Kluck's 2nd Army was within shelling range of Paris, and 800 of the city's taxis were assembling to ferry last-ditch French defenders to the front.

In the countryside around Authuille, rumours of the German advance were evolving almost hourly. The most current claims had the fighting at Maricourt, only five miles distant. The Vaquettes were one of just a handful of French families who decided to remain. The deployment in the village of French troops at mid-morning that day might have further stiffened their resolve, but Mme. Vaquette witnessed their arrival alone. Her husband had not returned.

By midday, there was still no sign of him, and French soldiers refused all access to the path he had followed that morning. At 3.00 p.m., Mme. Vaquette gathered together her children. In the early evening, a French sergeant arrived and broke the news that Boromée was dead. A young French sentry posted on the Thiepval plateau had mistaken the iron stakes and chains of his cows' enclosure for a defensive German position and shot him twice in the chest.[1] Not until nine days later, on a moonless night, could Vaquette's body be recovered from where it lay yards from the German lines, and be buried in the churchyard of Authuille.

Two years later, in the first light of 1 July, a British sniper of the King's Own Yorkshire Light Infantry (KOYLI) lay out mere yards from where the Somme's first victim had fallen. Private Ernest Deighton

---

1 Vaquette was killed on the horizon of Panorama **8**, to the right of the most conspicuous tractor tracks.

Front Line
250yds

THE NAB
X1690.00 1120yds

British Front Line
Tithebarn Street: 2nd Manchesters 650yds

OVILLERS
2200yds

S A L I E N T

L O C H

Hindenburg Street
300yds

Sanda Sap

POZIÈRES
3600yds

Enemy Front Line
650yds

M. G
X1a55.85 350yds

THE NORDWERK
X2679.05 2000yds

(whose story is recorded in Lyn Macdonald's excellent 1983 book *Somme*) was the first soldier in the no man's land of Thiepval that morning. Concealed on the edge of a shell-hole, Deighton had already accounted for two German sentries silhouetted by the dawn. It was the start of what would be a bloody day. At zero hour, when the first waves of British soldiers reached his position, Deighton would join them in the attack.

In front of the British lines here, on an eastward right angle, lay the Leipzig Salient with its twin German strongholds of the Wundt Werk (wonder work), a six-angled, star-shaped redoubt, and the Granatloch (shell-hole), 'a big, disused and very evil-looking quarry'. This protrusion in the German line invited a twin-pronged 'pincer' attack, but Divisional HQ thought such a manoeuvre beyond their greenhorn troops. Initially the assault was to be made from the west only, by the kilted ranks of the 16th (Glasgow Boys' Brigade) and 17th (Glasgow Commercials) battalions of the Highland Light Infantry.

The Commercials had spent the night of 29 June in huts on the hill at Bouzincourt alongside the British artillery batteries. The men were issued with cotton wool for earplugs, yet the survivors of the battle were nonetheless stone deaf for several days afterwards. They still somehow managed a stirring rendition of 'The Bonnie Banks o' Loch Lomond' as they marched to the front, a spectacle that greatly moved the French locals who witnessed it. It would be the last time the 'Old Seventeenth' sang their way into battle.

There is a long-standing belief that the Germans had a particular terror of Scottish regiments because of their alleged reluctance to take prisoners – and indeed, a Private R. Love of the 17th Highland Light Infantry was one of several to record that, in their battle orders for the morning of 1 July, the Glasgow men were explicitly told not to do so.[2] The Commercials spent the last hours before zero in a trench north of Campbell Avenue (from where Panorama ❽ was taken) opposite the Granatloch. The 16th HLI moved up to their left in front of the Wundt Werk, their ranks already significantly thinned over the previous two days. On the night of the 29th, a patrolling platoon was 'wiped out owing to an accident', and during a football match on the 30th, half the players were obliterated when a stray 5.9-inch German shell landed between the goalposts at the defending side's end.

Under the orders of Brigadier-General J. B. Jardine, at 7.23 a.m. the 17th HLI moved up the hill almost within shrapnel distance of the British barrage.[3] As the guns lifted at zero hour, they were less than 40 yards from the German lines. In under a minute, they were across the wire and into the Granatloch. The Germans surrendered while most

---

2 Such instructions, either explicit or implied, were far from unknown, but always verbal. Haig's Chief of Staff, Lieutenant-General Sir Lancelot Kiggell, went about as far as he could on paper with his directive of 28 June: 'It is the duty of all ranks to continue to use their weapons against the enemy's fighting troops, unless and until it is beyond all doubt that those have not only ceased all resistance, but that, whether having voluntarily thrown away their weapons or otherwise, they have definitely and finally abandoned all hope or intention of resisting further. In the case of apparent surrender, it lies with the enemy to prove his intention beyond the possibility of misunderstanding, before the surrender can be accepted as genuine.'

3 Jardine had observed the efficacy of this tactic, one used to great effect by the British as the war dragged on, while serving as a liaison officer with the Japanese during the 1904–5 Russo-Japanese War.

were still underground.[4] It was not until the Commercials pressed forward towards *Hindenburg Street* that they started to take severe casualties. To their left, large numbers of the 'men' of the 16th HLI – over half of whom were still in their teens – had been hit by machine-gun bullets within moments of leaving their trenches. By the time they reached the intact German wire, even more had been cut down by the Wundt Werk and Thiepval chateau Maxims at their optimum range of 300–400 yards. Within 30 minutes, 15 officers and 400 men had been killed or wounded.

In no man's land, Private Deighton still lay prone in his shell hole. Machine-gun rounds 'hissed as they crossed overhead'. Without turning, he could hear his fellow KOYLI men being hit as they finally neared his position. As the first Yorkshiremen drew alongside, Deighton got to his feet.

Many soldiers of the Great War afterwards described their first introduction to the din of battle as being abstracted and dream-like. F. P. Crozier observed that 'God is merciful and it almost seems as though he chloroforms us on these occasions.' The historian Denis Winter has judged that 'the one happening during an advance which seems to have had the power to break through a man's intense fixation on himself was the death of someone he knew close by'.

Now, seeing an old pal next to him machine-gunned through the chest, and himself shot in the shoulder from the same burst, Deighton made a frenzied charge into the German front line. He found a dugout 'full of Jerries' in *Hindenburg Street*. Pulling the pin from a Mills bomb with his teeth, he threw it amongst the terror-stricken men. Ignoring their agonies, he moved around the next traverse to find himself face to face with another German soldier. Unable to fire his rifle one-handed, he lunged bodily with his bayonet and impaled the man through the chest. 'Oh, I were wild. Seeing Clem like that,' he recalled. Making for the next line, he was hit a second time through the fingers; then a third. This time the bullet went through the rim of his helmet, then straight down and through his foot. Deighton's fight was over.

To the south, the 11th Borders (the Lonsdales),[5] volunteers from the wilds of Cumberland and Westmorland, had moved up from Crucifix Corner to their assembly trenches in Authuille Wood. Their task was to follow the Scotsmen into the Granatloch, and then advance to Mouquet Farm and capture the advance German HQ. This was their first battle, but they were under no illusions as to what lay ahead: on the night of 5 June, 75 Lonsdale soldiers had conducted a raid on the Leipzig Redoubt, and only half had returned. The battalion's 53-year-old commanding officer, Lieutenant-Colonel P. W. Machell (an old Empire soldier recruited by the Earl of Lonsdale from the neighbouring Crackenthorpe Hall, home of the Machell family since 1100), wrote an addendum to his final instructions: 'If it goes badly, I shall come up and see it through.'

4   Despite previous battle orders, these enemy soldiers were sent to the rear as prisoners. Some, however, were made to run through their own artillery barrage on the way.

5   So called as the battalion was raised and initially financed by the flamboyant 5th Earl of Lonsdale (1857–1944). Needled in the press for his pre-war friendship with the kaiser (Wilhelm had stayed at Lowther Castle for a week's grouse shooting in 1895), Lonsdale set about recruiting his unit with unparalleled gusto. The first men to enlist were given solid silver cap badges depicting a winged griffin from his family's coat of arms. Lonsdale's famous recruiting poster 'Are You a Man or Are You a Mouse?' caused some local controversy. When a local official arrived to complain, Lonsdale refused to see him. He was reportedly too busy designing the battalion's uniform, which somewhat counter-intuitively he intended – until Kitchener stopped him – to be coloured grey.

From their jump-off positions on the edge of the wood, the Borderers were unable to make out through the smoke of battle the progress of the Highland Light Infantrymen. They were also unaware that the 8th Division to their right across Nab Valley had failed to take the German stronghold of the Nordwerk on the Ovillers Spur. At 8.30 a.m., they therefore shook hands and went over.

'I set my teeth and jumped out of the trench and followed the rest in single file,' an unnamed nineteen-year-old member of B Company remembered. 'A machine gun somewhere opened out. A bullet burned at the back of my neck. TN, my best pal dropped. I looked back to see if he was wounded or what, he raised himself up on his hand, gave a smile and then dropped back – he gave a shudder, then lay still … This lad was only seventeen … We had barely gone another five yards when it seemed to rain bullets.'

Seeing the advancing soldiers cut down, Lieutenant-Colonel Machell rushed to the parapet to rally his men. Within yards, he was shot through the head. His adjutant, Lieutenant Gordon, was then severely injured himself as he attended the mortally wounded man. Advancing close to their beloved commander, Machell's bugler, batman and two runners were also killed, along with a seventeen-year-old private from Skelton, Thomas Hartness. His nineteen-year-old brother Private Richard Hartness witnessed his death. Richard himself was killed six weeks later.

Now without senior officers (Major Diggle, the second-in-command, was wounded as well), many men took cover in no man's land, among them the unnamed nineteen-year-old member of B Company. He noticed a bumblebee buzz once or twice round his head, then settle on a flower; also a soldier coming towards him, tearing at his tunic and screaming, 'Mother, mother.' 'I shut my eyes, expecting to feel his hands at my throat, but he ran past me towards the German trenches. The poor fellow must have went mad with pain or something.' Only a handful of Lonsdale soldiers joined the Scots and Yorkshiremen in the Granatloch.

While the battle to hold the quarry continued, and Private Deighton slipped in and out of consciousness beyond *Hindenburg Street*, the 14th Reserve Brigade were close behind the Lonsdales through Authuille Wood. 'It was apparent that matters were not progressing as favourably as had been anticipated,' the 1st Dorsets' official diary recorded. As the brigade moved up Dumbarton Track to the open sky, they stepped over scores of the Cumbrians' bodies. They now followed the same path as the Lonsdales, expecting no different result: 300 Dorsetshire and 268 Lancastrian soldiers duly became casualties on the slopes overlooked by the Nordwerk. The 15th HLI and 2nd Manchesters were awaiting their turn in the wings of Nab Valley.[6] They were now mercifully ordered to stand down.[7]

During the morning, fragments from no fewer than seven battalions had congregated in the Granatloch. For the rest of the day, this ragged

---

6   Later known by British soldiers as 'Blighty Valley' due to its resemblance to the peaceful fields of home.

7   From their trenches running from Tithebarn Street to Nab Valley, two platoons of the 2nd Manchesters did make it forward to the Granatloch at 1.45 p.m. Circumventing the Nordwerk machine guns through Authuille Wood, they filed up to the quarry via Sanda Sap, a covered tunnel that connected the position with the British front lines (see the relevant annotation on Panorama **8**).

Fold out for Panorama **9**: *Nab Valley*

group fought with desperate courage to hold on to their one gain. In the midst of this action (fought mainly by bomb-throwing), 32-year-old Sergeant James Youll Turnbull (17th HLI) won the 723rd Victoria Cross. An able cricketer with a famously long arm, Turnbull out-threw the Germans for over nine hours until, during a lull in the fighting, he was shot dead by a sniper. The attack north of Thiepval had faltered for want of supporting troops, but here, to the south of the village, there was simply no room for reinforcements. Four officers and over 700 dead, dying, wounded and desperately thirsty men occupied the 70 x 40 yard open white sepulchre of the redoubt. German shells, now immaculately aimed, landed like giant hammers in a butcher's shop. Yet the soldiers from Yorkshire, Lancashire, Cumberland, Manchester and Dorset and the men and boys from Glasgow held on. By the end of the day, they could record a victory amidst a landscape of defeat: the conquest of a large hole of chalk 300 yards away from where they started. It was the

greatest territorial gain of the northern battlefield, coming at the cost of over 2,500 men killed or wounded. The British military would headline it in their account of the day.

Private Ernest Deighton remained a helpless witness to the battle. Without food, water or hope of recovery, he lay in a shell hole for four days. His two wounded companions died. He used the body of one of them to screen himself from machine-gun fire. On 5 July, hearing the sound of advancing British soldiers, Deighton made a last bid for survival. Crawling 500 yards with one serviceable arm and leg, he fell head first into the British lines. He was capable of only one word: 'Orange.' Recognising it as the password for the men of the 1 July attack, stretcher-bearers carried him down to a dressing station in Nab Valley. The first man onto the battlefield had been the last man off it. The KOYLI medical officer, Captain Marshall, received him with surprise and resignation. 'Good God! This is eighty-seven in now. That'll be it, then,' he said.

made at c. 7.30 am. BST on c. 1st July 2015 from *N E of Mersey St : 2nd Manchesters 7.30 am BST 1st July 1916*

including a field view of *128°* from about **NW** to **ESE**

Approximate Scale of Degrees (1 degree equals *2/5* inches).

| 2 | 3 | 4 | 5 | 6 | 7 | 8 | 9 | 10 | 11 | 12 |

MARTINPUICH
7000 yds

POZIÈRES
2800 yds

COURCELETTE
5700 yds

M. G.
X2a 73. 60 630 yds

Cemetery
X4a 40. 99

Enemy 2nd Line
580 yds

Brimstone Trench
1350 yds

M. G.
X2a 28. 42 350 yds

THE NORDWERK
X2a 79. 05 1080 yds
M.G. M.G. M.G. M.G.

Line

Skyline Trench
1300 yds

FC

Pa

0

Y

FF REDOUBT
R 21 c 4. 9 3400 yds

Mouquet Farm
R 33 63. 8 2000 yds

Pear Trench
700 yds

Daniel's Den
570 yds

Enemy

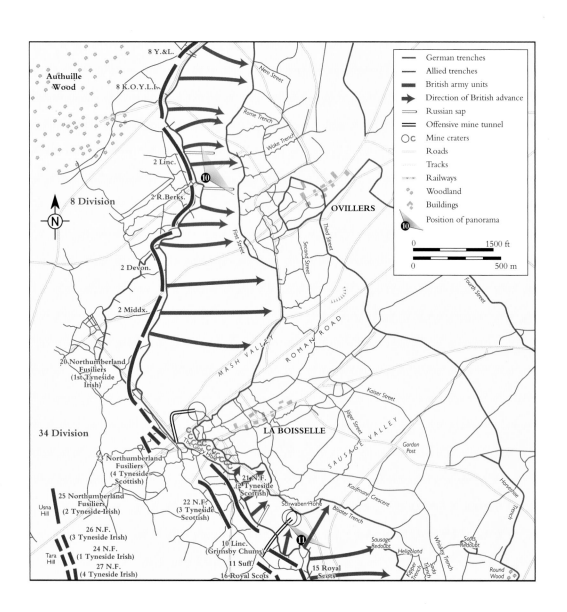

Authuille
Wood

8 Y.&L.

8 K.O.Y.L.I.

Nero Street

Rome Trench

Wake Trench

2 Linc.

10

2 R.Berks.

OVILLERS

8 Division

N

First Street

Second Street

Third Street

2 Devon.

2 Middx.

Fourth Street

MASH VALLEY

ROMAN ROAD

20 Northumberland
Fusiliers
(1st Tyneside
Irish)

Kaiser Street

34 Division

Jäger Street

SAUSAGE VALLEY

Gordon
Post

23 Northumberland
Fusiliers
(4 Tyneside
Scottish)

LA BOISSELLE

The Glory Hole

25 Northumberland
Fusiliers
(2 Tyneside Irish)

21 N.F.
(2 Tyneside
Scottish)

Usna
Hill

Kaufmann Crescent

22 N.F.
(3 Tyneside
Scottish)

Schwaben Höhe

Bloater Trench

26 N.F.
(3 Tyneside Irish)

Horseshoe Trench

24 N.F.
(1 Tyneside Irish)

Sausage
Redoubt

Scots
Redoubt

Tara
Hill

10 Linc.
(Grimsby Chums)

11

Heligoland

Whiskey Trench

27 N.F.
(4 Tyneside Irish)

11 Suff.

Soda
Trench

Round
Wood

16 Royal Scots

15 Royal
Scots

Kipper
Trench

──	German trenches
──	Allied trenches
▬	British army units
➤	Direction of British advance
═	Russian sap
═	Offensive mine tunnel
○c	Mine craters
	Roads
	Tracks
	Railways
	Woodland
	Buildings
10	Position of panorama

0   1500 ft

0   500 m

CHAPTER 7

OVILLERS & LA BOISSELLE

'If the first attack goes well,' General Haig wrote in a message to General Sir Henry Rawlinson, Commander of 4th Army, on 21 June, 'every effort must be made to develop the success to the utmost by firstly opening a way for our cavalry and then as quickly as possible pushing the cavalry through to seize Bapaume.' It was here, at the centre of the battlefield, that Haig wanted his breakthrough. He confided to the Chief of the Imperial General Staff, General Sir William Robertson, that he intended to use his mounted divisions 'on the lines of 1806' – that is, like Napoleon did at Jena, where the French cavalry had turned an initial infantry break-in into a rout of the Prussian forces. Whenever he was spared the more measured vision of his subordinates, the British commander-in-chief allowed himself the hope that General Gough's horsemen would do the same.

The region north of the Somme had seen many military spectacles down the ages. In 57 BC, Caesar's legionaries had marched down their own road from Bapaume to Albert on the hunt for recalcitrant Gauls. In 1415, Henry V's knights and bowmen crossed the Somme en route from Harfleur to their victory at Agincourt. And four centuries later, a regiment of the Duke of Wellington's army had passed through in pursuit of fragments of the French Imperial Guard fleeing from their ruin at Waterloo.

But these were armies of hundreds who had fought their battles by appointment, using swords, lances and then muzzle-loaded flintlocks. This time, the invaders had come in tens of thousands, lugging with them industrial machines that would do their killing for them. The vision of battle as a noble, swashbuckling enterprise was over. Joseph Glidden and Hiram Maxim – inventors of barbed wire and the machine gun – had seen to that.[1] Before the cavalry could now take to the field of battle, the attacking infantry had to defeat the defenders, who held all the technological trumps. Not a single horse would therefore go into battle on 1 July.

The line from Ovillers to La Boisselle was taken over from the French by the British in the autumn of 1915. The trenches that the British inherited were notoriously awful. Not only was the ground prone to flooding, but front-line home improvements were actively discouraged by the British High Command, as they had been by the French. The official line was that forward positions were to be viewed as strictly temporary – staging posts on an inexorable advance – and that the front-line troops should not make themselves too comfortable. The French on the Somme had followed these instructions closely. When the British arrived at La Boisselle, they found the trenches either collapsing, waterlogged or covered in brambles. Some of the line didn't even join up.

---

1   Granted their US Patents in 1874 (no. 157124) and 1885 (no. 321513) respectively.

1. Panoramas are taken solely for military purposes.
2. The publication of them in the press will necessarily give valuable information to the enemy.
3. This panorama is to be kept with as much security as is compatible with full advantage of it being taken by our own troops.
4. When troops are relieved this panorama should be handed over to the relieving troops.

Nero Street 750 yds

ne Trench 480 yds

THE NORDWERK X2b79. 05 2000 yds

M.G. X2c72.30 700 yds

Enemy Fourth Line 980 yds

Enemy Third Line 610 yds

Enemy Second Line 330 yds

Enemy Front L.. 230 yds

FOURTH ARMY.

Map

Panorama No. *10* made at *c.7.30 a.m BST* on *c.1st July 2015* from *E of Ulverston Trench : 2nd Royal Berkshire Regiment 7.30am BST 1st July*

including a field view of *122°* from about *N N W* to *E S E*

Approximate Scale of Degrees (1 degree equals *2/5* inches).

| 0 | 1 | 2 | 3 | 4 | 5 | 6 | 7 | 8 | 9 | 10 |

THIEPVAL
2500 yds

NAB VALLEY
1070 yds

M. G.
X 76 89. 90 330 yds

M. G.
X 76 85. 84 300 yds

Charles Douie, a young nineteen-year-old subaltern with the 1st Dorsets,[2] arriving in early 1916, described the scene: 'We passed down our front-line trench towards the ruins of the cemetery through which our line ran. Here there were only sand-bags, one layer thick, and about two feet above the top of the all-prevailing mud … Liquid slime washed over and above our knees. The shattered crosses of the cemetery lay at every angle about the torn graves, while one cross, still erect by some miracle, overlooked the craters and ruins of La Boisselle. Death, indeed, was emperor here.'

Its empire grew with the arrival of the British. The laxness of the line's former tenants was anathema to British commanders. Keen to look busy, they at once increased the activity of artillery and snipers – provoking German retaliation that resulted in scores of men being killed. The number of patrols and raids also increased. These nocturnal exercises were intended to gather intelligence, but had little effect other than prompting the Germans to reinforce whichever part of their line the British intended to assault later. The returning raiders, breathlessly whispering their passwords, were also quite often shot by their own side. On the pretext of training men in the fighting spirit and blooding inexperienced officers, the High Command, however, continued to insist on these 'minor trench operations' for the duration of the war – a confusion of soldiers with foxhounds that would kill thousands of the army's best-in-battle before a battle had even begun.

In front of Ovillers and in Mash Valley, battalion commanders knew by the fourth day of the preliminary bombardment that the coming battle would dwarf the cost of any trench raid. Here the distance between the opposing front lines was over 700 yards, the greatest width of no man's land on the whole front. It was open ground and well observed from both the fortified villages, which were 'all be-Boched and mined and enfiladed, as well as trenched and ranged on, till they were as strong as death.'[3] The British could see that the German wire stood as well each morning as it had the previous day. And a raiding party at Ovillers had reported hearing singing from a German dugout.

Lieutenant-Colonel Edwin Sandys, the 40-year-old CO of the 2nd Middlesex, had agonised over the sight of the still-intact German positions for six sleepless nights. On the eve of the battle, he raised his reservations with his superiors. He was met with a conspiracy of denial. General Rawlinson had made clear that 'all criticism by subordinates … of orders received by superior authority will, in the end, recoil on the heads of the critics.' In the face of any disquieting evidence, senior commanders therefore invariably 'raised a telescope to a patched eye' rather than suffer any 'recoil' themselves. Some of the top brass were more candid. On 30 June, Major-General Ingouville-Williams ('Inky Bill'), commander of the 34th Division, took a party of NCOs from the Grimsby Chums to a front-line trench[4] and pointed to the ridge beyond *Sausage Valley*. 'I am willing to sacrifice the whole of the 101st Brigade to

----

2   Author of *The Weary Road: Recollections of a Subaltern of Infantry* (1929).

3   John Masefield, *Letters from the Front 1915–17* (1984).

4   The position from which Panorama **11** was taken.

Fold out for Panorama **10**: *Ovillers*

'take that,' he told them. By the end of the next day, he very nearly had – but without taking the ridge.

By contrast, directly in front of La Boisselle, the British and German trenches were only 50 yards apart. In between lay a stinking scrapyard of mine craters, ordnance and human remains known by British soldiers as the Glory Hole. The assaulting troops would avoid it, attacking in a pincer movement to either side of the village. The advance was to be signalled by the detonation of two huge mines: Y Sap to the north of the Roman Road, and Lochnagar[5] to the south. The shaft of the Lochnagar tunnel was sunk 100 yards behind the British front line by 185 Tunnelling Company on 11 November 1915. Initially sloping diagonally downwards, it levelled out at a depth of 50 feet to a 4 ft 6 in x 2 ft 6 in gallery driven underneath the German stronghold of the Schwaben Höhe. As at Hawthorn Ridge, the excavation was carried out in breath-holding silence. The miners worked barefoot on a carpet of sandbags, prising out 18 inches of chalk every 24 hours. They could often hear German miners in a transversal tunnel 30 feet below them. Yet the British miners at Lochnagar maintained their secrecy. To the 9 officers and 315 men manning the German line above the chambers, the detonation of 60,000 lbs of ammonal on 1 July came as a complete surprise.

The unease of local commanders was not for the most part contagious. As the men of the 8th and 34th divisions marched up to their lines that stretched from The Nab to Bécourt, spirits were high. Some even took time to savour the aesthetics. 'The enemy trenches look very pretty sometimes in the sunlight,' recorded Major W. A. Vignoles of the 10th Lincolns as he rested on a discarded plough; 'our shells bursting over them in yellow, black or white puffs. Many are covered with a bright yellow weed, while between the heavy white lines of chalk, there are frequently large fields of brilliant scarlet poppies.' The sight of the bombardment and the waiting cavalry made many cheer in the belief that the moment of the breakthrough had come. On hearing of the division's objectives, a Corporal S. F. Hill of the 34th Signal Company packed an extra pair of boots in his haversack. 'They needed attention, and I expected to be able to get them repaired in Bapaume,' he said.

Other soldiers, quite frequently older ones, could not share their comrades' optimism. They wrote, prayed or 'communicated only with themselves'. Some went further. On hearing rumours that the Germans were waiting for the attack, a man from the 11th Suffolks shot himself in the kneecap. 'He had pluck, I think,' stated another Suffolk. 'It was a strange sight to see him carried away on a stretcher under arrest, with a man at each side of him with fixed bayonets. I often wonder what happened to him.'[6] The rumours were not unfounded. The Germans *were* ready. In the early hours of 1 July, they would be made readier still.

5 The mine took its name from a trench near to the tunnel shaft, itself christened after the famous peak on Royal Deeside by an officer of the 7th Gordons in the summer of 1915. A number of men who had enlisted in the battalion were previously workers on the Balmoral estate.

6 In the list of the 346 men who were executed by firing squad during the war, there is no record of a soldier from the 11th Suffolks. We can therefore assume that this self-wounded soldier was either one of 17,000 others convicted of charges carrying the death penalty, yet who did not receive a capital sentence, or one of 2,654 men whose death sentences were later commuted.

S

CONTALMAISON
3250 yds

Roman Road to Bapaume
1450 yds

Contalmaison Wood
R10c8.2 2450 yds

M. G.
X8d82.38 700 yds

M. G.
X8a05.18 250 yds

Street
ds

Third Street
630 yds

Fourth Street
980 yds

O V I L L

POZIÈRES
1850 yds

M.G.
X2d 42.29 950yds

Wake Trench
480 yds

Western Trench
2300 yds

Howitzer Avenue
2700 yds

Spring Gardens
1300 yds

Smyth Alley
2100 yds

First Stree
230 yds

At 10.17 p.m. on 30 June, General Rawlinson sent a final communiqué to all units of the 4th Army: 'In wishing all ranks good luck, the Army Commander desires to impress on all infantry units the supreme importance of helping one another and holding on tight to every yard of ground gained. The accurate and sustained fire of the artillery ... should greatly assist the task of the infantry.' Though not a Churchillian message, a staff officer still thought it important enough to be transmitted over the expressly forbidden field telephone. The German Moritz 28 North listening station housed in a La Boisselle cellar picked it up shortly after 2.00 a.m. The news was transmitted along the enemy line: the British were coming that morning.

In the hour before zero, a team of Royal Engineers put the finishing touches to their record-breaking weapon 50 feet below the German front lines to the south of the village. They were taking no chances. No fewer than twelve detonators, each with a guncotton primer, were distributed on each of the two charges. A reserve set of detonators was also connected. A wire was then unrolled back along the gallery to a dugout at the shaft entrance and attached to a small wooden box. A wooden-handled brass plunger, similar to the flusher on a Thunderbox lavatory, extended through a hole in the top. At 7.28 a.m., Captain James Young pressed it briskly downwards. The serrated-tooth pinion turned the generator, from which an electrical pulse reached the detonators in less than half a second. Early-morning walkers on Hampstead Heath heard the result.

Second Lieutenant Cecil Lewis of the 3rd Squadron of the Royal Flying Corps was flying overhead: 'The whole earth heaved and flashed ... there was an ear-splitting roar, drowning all the guns, flinging the machine sideways in the repercussing air. The earth column rose higher and higher to almost 4,000 feet. There it hung, or seemed to hang, for a moment in the air, like the silhouette of some great cypress tree, then fell away in a widening cone of dust and debris.'

The men of the first waves in front of the crater (measuring 300 ft across and 90 ft deep) had been told to wait five minutes for the spoil to subside. It was four minutes too long. When the 10th Lincolns and 2nd Tyneside Scottish went over, their progress east was impeded not by falling chalk but by German MG 08 machine-gun rounds. Some of the defending Badeners held their fire until the British soldiers were less than 20 yards away. They then annihilated the advancing Tommies in a concert of rifle and machine-gun fire. A number of men were hit on the lip of the crater – still 'as hot as an oven' – and accumulated in a pile at the bottom.

The Württembergers of Infanterie Regiment 180 at Ovillers were not so patient. During the final intensive salvoes of the bombardment, they had not even bothered to take cover. Their machine guns began raking the British parapets fifteen minutes before zero hour even as the 2nd Lincs, 2nd Berks and 2nd Devons tried to halve their attack distance under the barrage. Seventy Lincolnshire men made it briefly to the German second line and held on to the first for an hour (during which their commander, Lieutenant-Colonel Reginald Bastard, went back across no man's land to rally reinforcements) before they were forced to withdraw.

In *Mash Valley*, Lieutenant-Colonel Sandys of the 2nd Middlesex confirmed his worst fears through his binoculars. Although the Germans had remained ignorant of the Lochnagar mine, they had evacuated

Y Sap. And so close were the British lines to La Boisselle that the British artillery had only gingerly bombarded the south of the village. Most of the shells hadn't exploded anyway. One officer noted a dud every two or three yards over several acres of ground. Some men did cross the 750 yards to the German front trenches, but were turned out again within minutes. Most lay dead or wounded along the way. At 8.00 a.m., Sandys followed his men into the valley. He was wounded four times, including losing a toe, before a bullet to his right thigh forced him to be carried to the rear. An artillery officer watched Sandys's battalion march away from the battlefield that evening. There was one officer and 28 men.

On the far left of the 8th Division's assault just south of the Nab, men of the 8th King's Own Yorkshire Light Infantry and the 8th Yorks and Lancs initially made some progress. Advancing in the lee of the hill, they reached the first lines of German trenches.[7] But just as the Nordwerk machine gunners had slaughtered the Lonsdales on the Thiepval plateau, the machine gunners of the Granatloch now massacred the Yorkshire and Lancashire volunteers on the Ovillers Spur. The 9th Yorks and Lancs followed on schedule, among them Corporal J. H. Tansley: 'We had been told, "There's no need for this short rushes and getting down on your stomach, go straight over as if you were on parade."' In so doing, Tansley and his best pal were shot simultaneously. 'I attended to my mate and he had some qualms of conscience in him, because he wasn't facing the enemy when he went down. I didn't realise anything like that myself, but he was an old regular soldier and it troubled him so much.' Tansley's friend didn't fret long. Seconds later he was shot through the mouth.

For the civilian soldiers, 1 July was their first introduction to the sheer volume of battle. Even when otherwise unscathed, some soldiers' ears bled from the percussive effect of shells bursting nearby. One sound amidst the fighting at La Boisselle, however, was more familiar. 'The pluckiest thing I ever saw,' remembered an officer of the 2nd Middlesex, 'was a piper of the Tyneside Scottish playing his company over the parapet … The last glimpse I had of him … showed him still marching erect, playing furiously, and quite regardless of the flying bullets and the men dropping all around him.' The man was Pipe Major John Wilson of the 20th Northumberland Fusiliers, and he survived the battle. His uncle, Lance Corporal Pipe Garnet Wolseley Fyfe, of the same battalion, didn't. 'I did see poor "Aggy" Fyfe,' recalled a fellow Tynesider. 'He was riddled with bullets and screaming. Another lad was just kneeling, his head thrown right back. Bullets were just slapping into him knocking great bloody chunks off his body.'

Such were the numbers of wounded men that the task of the stretcher-bearers was hopeless. Ordinary soldiers frequently rescued their stricken comrades themselves. Fifty yards in front of the British front line to the north of the crater, Private Tom Easton of the 2nd Tyneside Scottish was granted permission to recover the badly wounded Sergeant Wear. 'I got these two or three lads and we got a groundsheet. We couldn't carry him. We trailed him on the sheet. We laid him down for a bit of a rest and he said, "I don't know what the bloody hell you're bothering about me for. I'm half bloody dead anyway."' They told him they were going to bother. With shells bursting steadily overhead, the

---

7 *Daniel's Den* and *Pear Trench*, indicated in Panorama **9**.

FOURTH ARMY.

Panorama No. *11* made at *c.7.30 am.B.S.T.* on *c.1st July 2015* from *End of Pocran St.: 10th Lincolns (Grimsby Chums) 7.30 a.m.*

including a field view of *144°* from about *N.N.W.* to *E.S.E.*

Approximate Scale of Degrees (1 degree equals *1/3* inches).

| 0 | 1 | 2 | 3 | 4 | 5 | 6 | 7 | 8 | 9 | 10 |

M A S H   V A L L E Y

S C H

LA BOISSELLE

M.G.
R.20a 79.41 260 yds

M.G.
R.14a 31.24 1440 yds

OVILLER
2000 yds

The Glory Hole
350 yds   *M.G.*
R.14c 19.65 1075 yds

Enemy Front Line
380 yds

three Northumberlands dragged Wear to the British lines. Their greatest obstacle was other wounded British soldiers. 'We were absolutely trampling on them. You couldn't help it. It's bad enough when you're getting bloody wounded, but it's bloody murder when they're trampling on you as well. Oh, they were crying out! I can hear them now. But there wasn't a thing we could do about it.' Sergeant Wear died later that day.

While the German defenders, 'grinning at their officers with pipes in their mouths', shot down the oncoming British waves in front of the crater, the 15th and 16th Scots on the right flank made an extravagant advance. The ridge on the horizon of the battlefield is a long pull up even in modern peacetime, but 'Pontius Pilate's Bodyguard'[8] reached Birch Tree Wood by 8.15 a.m. Thrust southwards by the weight of machine-gun fire from the top of *Sausage Valley*,[9] they attacked towards Peake Woods to correct the line of their advance, but were driven back. A wounded captain of the 11th Suffolks marshalled the remnants of three battalions for an assault on *Scots Redoubt*. They took it, and for once were thankful for the inadequacies of the British artillery, which had left the position's defences undamaged. The men held on until water and ammunition were brought up that night from the British lines through Round Wood. It was the 8th and 34th divisions' most significant consolidated gain of the day.

But the folklore of the battle would belong to the Tyneside Irishmen. Though the 103rd was technically a support brigade at the rear of the British formation, its four battalions were ordered to rise from their trenches on the Usna and Tara hills at the same moment as the leading waves. A tribal brotherhood of northeastern coal men, fathers and sons among them, they marched on in 'beautifully dressed lines' with rifles at the slope, bayonets glinting above their heads in the sunlight.[10] In places, the men were 1,500 yards behind the British front line, and most were killed or wounded by the falling bullets of a German machine-gun barrage before they got to it.

Some men from the 27th Northumberlands also joined the fight for *Scots Redoubt* and assisted in holding the line there. Isolated bands under a Major S. Acklom occupied *Jäger Street* and *Kaufmann Crescent* before withdrawing to the British lines in mid-afternoon. The German defenders took photographs of their retreat. But in a miracle of endurance not believed possible by senior officers, a party of fourteen Northumberland Fusiliers, including a Private George Lowery from Crook in County Durham, made it to the village of Contalmaison itself, over 4,200 yards from their jump-off point. It was the furthest advance by any British soldiers that day.

Over the course of the day's fighting, approximately 4,000 defenders had manned the German line at Ovillers and La Boisselle. At Ovillers, the total casualties sustained by two German battalions amounted to 276 men. More than 19,000 British soldiers had attacked between the

---

8 Nickname for The Royal Scots (The Royal Regiment), once known as the Royal Regiment of Foot, the oldest and most senior infantry regiment of the line of the British Army. Raised in 1633 during the reign of Charles I, the regiment existed continuously until 2006 when it merged with other Scottish units to form the Royal Regiment of Scotland.

9 So called after a German observation balloon that hung over the area. The adjacent valley to the north west inevitably became *Mash*.

10 A number of these soldiers appeared to be carrying two rifles, but the second was in fact the shaft of an entrenching tool. They had put its heavy metal blade down their tunic and breeches as improvised body armour.

Fold out for Panorama **11**: *La Boisselle*

Nab and Bécourt that morning. By nightfall, 11,501 of them were dead, wounded or missing. Major-General Ingouville-Williams's 34th had taken the greatest divisional losses (6,380) on the whole front, while eleven British battalions had each suffered more than 500 casualties. Out of 729 men of the 4th Tyneside Scottish who went over, only 100 answered the roll the following day.[10] The old Roman road had been regarded as the main axis of the assault on 1 July. It was now the bloodiest ground on Britain's bloodiest day.

In the days following the battle, Lieutenant-Colonel Sandys was transported back to England to recover from his wounds. On 4 September, he went up to London and took a room at the Cavendish Hotel in Jermyn Street. On the morning of the 6th, he addressed a note to a brother officer, Captain William Lloyd Jones, ending with the words: 'I have never had a moment's peace since July 1st.' He then lay on his bed with his service revolver and fired a bullet through the roof of his mouth.[11]

* * *

The site of the Lochnagar Crater, used for years by fly tippers and cross-country motorbikes, was bought in 1978 by an Englishman, Richard Dunning. The memorial cross visible in Panorama ⑪ was erected by Dunning in 1986. It is constructed of reclaimed timber from a Gateshead church. The site attracts about 200,000 visitors a year. An annual memorial service is held at the site on 1 July, during which poppy petals are scattered into the crater.

10 The Tyneside Scottish had been refused the right to wear traditional Scottish battledress in 1914. Following the battle, however, the surviving men were given a small square of tartan to wear behind their cap badge as a tribute to their bravery, prompting Private Easton to remark: 'Man, we'll have to fight a lot of battles before we get wuh kilts.'

11 When the police were called, they found a bullet in the ceiling and Sandys still conscious. Taken to St George's Hospital, he was asked how many times he had discharged the gun. He held up one finger and gave his name. He died on 13 September 1916 from septic meningitis and a cerebral abscess caused by the wound. At the inquest, the jury returned a verdict of suicide during temporary insanity.

1. Panoramas are taken solely for military purposes.

2. The publication of them in the press will necessarily give valuable information to the enemy.

3. This panorama is to be kept with as much security as is compatible with full advantage of it being taken by our own troops.

4. When troops are relieved this panorama should be handed over to the relieving troops.

Round Wood
R21d4.4 1300yds

...ke Woods
. 7 1900yds

Scots Redoubt
R21c9.9 990yds
M.G.s

The Dingle
R27b2.9 1230yds

Shelter Wood
R22o2.2 1630yds

Horseshoe Trench
1280 yds

Birch Tree Wood
R21d8.6 1500yds

Whiskey Trench
890yds

Sausage Redoubt
R20d93. 94 530yds
M.G.s

Heligoland
R21c11.92 625yds
M.G.s

Soda Trench
790yds

The Crucifex
R28a.35.45 1900yds

Kipper Trench
610yds

SAUSAGE VALLEY

Kaufmann Crescent
510 yds

ater Trench
325 yds

Contalmaison Wood
R10c8.2 2600 yds

Gordon Post
R14d.95.19 720 yds

Bailiff Wood
R16a5.2 2150 yds

M.G.
R21a 20.91 820 yds

CONTALMAISON
2700 yds

Enemy Front Lin
410 yds

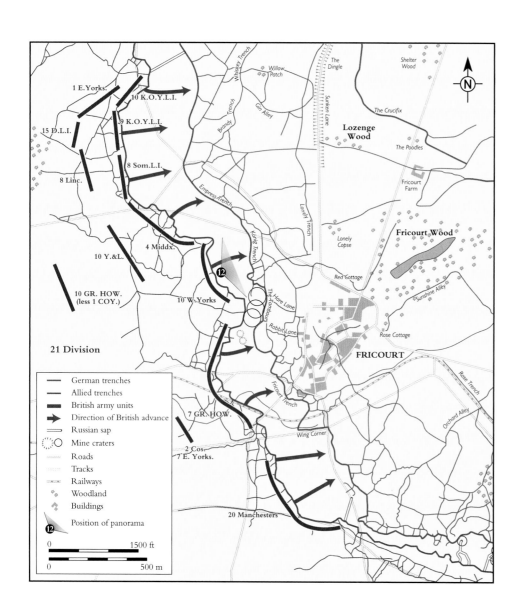

N

1 E.Yorks.

10 K.O.Y.L.I.

15 D.L.I.

9 K.O.Y.L.I.

8 Som.L.I.

8 Linc.

4 Middx.

10 Y.&L.

10 GR. HOW.
(less 1 COY.)

10 W.Yorks

21 Division

7 GR. HOW.

2 Cos.
7 E. Yorks.

20 Manchesters

Whiskey Trench

Willow
Patch

The
Dingle

Shelter
Wood

Brandy Trench

Gin Alley

Sunken Lane

The Crucifix

Lozenge
Wood

The Poodles

Fricourt
Farm

Empress Trench

Lonely Trench

Fricourt Wood

King Trench

Lonely
Copse

Red Cottage

Sunshine Alley

The Tambour

Hare Lane

Rabbit Lane

Rose Cottage

FRICOURT

Fricourt Trench

Wing Corner

Rose Trench

Orchard Alley

German trenches
Allied trenches
British army units
Direction of British advance
Russian sap
Mine craters
Roads
Tracks
Railways
Woodland
Buildings
Position of panorama

0   1500 ft

0   500 m

12

CHAPTER 8

FRICOURT

The assault on the village of Fricourt was watched by the most distinguished literary figure of the First World War. Commissioned as a second lieutenant in the Royal Welch Fusiliers in May 1915, Siegfried Sassoon had been on the Western Front for over a year, known as much for his reckless bravery as for his new 'no truth unfitting' brand of verse. Three weeks into the Battle of the Somme, he was awarded the Military Cross for gallantry. A year later, he would throw it into the sea.

The Royal Welch Fusiliers were in non-combatant reserve for the first day's attack. Nonetheless, Sassoon spent the morning of 30 June cutting holes on the German wire, an escapade he found 'by no means disagreeable'. 'It was rather like going out to weed a neglected garden after being warned that there might be a tiger among the gooseberry bushes,' he wrote. Later, as troops crammed into the support trench outside his dugout, he passed a staff officer named Durley wearing well-cut riding boots. ' "I suppose those brass-hats do know a hell of a lot about it all, don't they, Julian?" ' Sassoon ventured. 'Durley replied that he hoped they'd learnt something since last autumn when they'd allowed the infantry to educate themselves at Loos. "They've got to learn their job as they go along, like the rest of us," ' the staff officer added as he hurried to rejoin his horse.

In the battle for Fricourt, there would be a hint of tactical progress, but not enough to outweigh yet more record-breaking losses. History sometimes describes battalions being 'wiped out' on 1 July. In the case of the 10th West Yorkshire Regiment at Fricourt, this is only a slight exaggeration. Advancing to the north of the village, no more than twenty of the Yorkshire Pals managed to get through a cat's cradle of German machine-gun fire. It was established that evening that out of the 750 soldiers that had gone over, 710 were dead, wounded or missing – the highest casualty rate (at 95 per cent) of any battalion on 1 July, or indeed of any British battalion on a single day during the whole war.

It could have been even worse. While the British bombardment failed to subdue the defenders inside the village, the batteries of General Congreve's XIII Corps had at least undermined the German artillery. The machine gun has gone down in history as the 'skull and crossbones' weapon of the Somme battle, yet artillery claimed far more lives on 1 July, and soldiers lived in greatest terror of shellfire.[1] While there was a

---

1 Ernst Jünger (1895–1998), the German soldier, author and veteran of the Somme, offered the following insight in *Storms of Steel* (1920): 'You must imagine you are securely tied to a post, being menaced by a man swinging a heavy hammer. Now the hammer has been taken back over his head, ready to be swung, now it's cleaving the air towards you, on the point of touching your skull, then it's struck the post, and the splinters are flying — that's what it's like to experience heavy shelling in an exposed position.'

12

Fricourt Farm
X28c3.8 1020yds

The Poodles
X28a32.19 1150yds

Lonely Trench
600yds

König Trench
M.G. M.G.
F3a55.28 F3a56.18
270yds 270yds

Shelter Wood
R22c2.2 1550yds

The Crucifix
X28a32.19 1150yds

FOURTH ARMY.   Map

Panorama No. *12* made at *c730am BST* on *c1st July 2015* from *S of Tangier Trench : 10th West Yorkshire Regiment 730am BST 1st July 1916*

including a field view of *125°* from about **NNE** to **SE**

Approximate Scale of Degrees (1 degree equals *2/5* inches).

| 0 | 1 | 2 | 3 | 4 | 5 | 6 | 7 | 8 | 9 | 10 |

Whiskey Trench
1150 yds

Brandy Trench
820 yds

Empress Trench
440 yds

Willow Patch
X 27a 56.82 1100 yds

Enemy Front Line
280 yds

Round Wood
R21d4.4 1550 yds

Gin Alley
920 yds

The Dingle
R27c2.9 1350 yds

Birch Tree Wood
R21d8.6 1650 yds

Sunken Lane
920 yds

perceived 'cleanness' to a bullet wound – it would either kill instantly or with luck dispense a reasonably presentable 'blighty one' – soldiers knew only too well that shell fragments could cut them in half, or worse still obliterate them entirely. For a generation for whom the ritual of burial was an article of faith, the fear of dying *sine corpore* was the greatest of all.

In the trenches west of the village before zero hour, the waiting British soldiers were relieved to find the weight of the artillery falling mostly on the enemy. Fricourt was the knee in the leg of the battle front. Lieutenant-General Henry Sinclair Horne, the XV Corps commander, resolved to smash it by using twice his allocation of shells. The 21st and 7th divisions would then flank the ruins to the north and east before a further attack delivered the *coup de grâce* some time that afternoon.

On the evening of 29 June, the officers of the 9th King's Own Yorkshire Light Infantry gathered for a final dinner in La Neuville before the battle. The battalion had a bruised recent history. After suffering grievous casualties at Loos the previous autumn, its morale had not improved under the continuing command of Lieutenant-Colonel C. W. D. Lynch. A pedantic disciplinarian with an exalted military background, he had failed to endear himself to either the men or the 'temporary gentlemen' with whom he shared the mess. When urged to propose a toast to his CO, a Captain G. Haswell had refused, and when pressed, Haswell demonstrably fudged it: 'Gentlemen, I give you the King's Own Yorkshire Light Infantry, and in particular the 9th Battalion of the regiment.' There was a silence, which after

a moment Captain Haswell filled with a toast that would pass into military folklore: 'Gentlemen, when the barrage lifts…'[2]

Two other KOYLI men also shared a last reunion on the 29th, a less lavish affair in the village of Carnoy. Private Dick King and his brother Frank (also a private) were Nottinghamshire men who had followed the thicker coal seams to South Yorkshire. They had enlisted in Pontefract in August 1914. 'Here comes Kitchener's Army,' Dick had announced, arriving home late one day for tea. With the postponement of the battle, the Kings were granted leave to meet a third brother from the Royal Engineers. Together, they spent the evening drinking plonk in a local estaminet. As darkness fell, Frank moved to leave, but Dick insisted on staying. He returned to the battalion only just in time for reveille. The brothers, though separated, now found themselves in the forward trenches of the attack due east of Bécourt. Dick was unaware that his newly born daughter, Gladys Hope Verdun, would be christened in Yorkshire at St Mary's Church, Tickhill, later that afternoon.

Also in the first wave to the south was a 21-year-old law graduate from Sheffield. Second Lieutenant Philip Howe, whose remarkable story was preserved by Martin Middlebrook in *First Day on the Somme* (1971), had enlisted as a private in 1914 before going on to obtain a commission. He was a popular officer, made more so that morning by recovering the rum ration that had gone missing in transit. As the minutes ticked by, his eyes were trained to his right. As he and the 22 other officers of the

2 On 1 July 1921, the following entry appeared in the In Memoriam column of *The Times*: '9th AND 10th BNS., K.O.Y.L.I. – To the undying memory of the Officers and Men of the above Battalions who fell in the attack on Fricourt (Somme) on July 1, 1916. "Gentleman, when the barrage lifts."' The same entry famously appeared in the column on the anniversary of the battle for the next 65 years. Among the officers who fell were Lynch and Haswell, both killed on the approach to *Empress Trench* that morning. They lie buried almost side by side in Plot 1, Row B of Norfolk Cemetery, Bécordel-Bécourt.

 Fold out for Panorama 12: *Fricourt*

battalion knew, the detonation of three mines in the Tambour crater field would signal the attack. Protected by the spoil from the explosions, the battalion was to advance through *König Trench* and throw up a defensive screen to the north of the village. To their left, the 64th Brigade would pass through *Empress Trench* and complete the encirclement of the village south of *The Crucifix*. The plan was sophisticated in comparison with those prepared for other New Army units. But the soldiers were well drilled, and Second Lieutenant Howe had implicit faith in the men of his battalion. They were the volunteer pals from Leeds and Harrogate of the 10th West Yorks.

As the clock reached zero hour, Siegfried Sassoon left his dugout southwest of Wing Corner. His diaries relate: 'The air vibrates with the incessant din – the whole air rocks and shakes and throbs – it is one continuous roar. Machine guns tap and rattle, bullets whistling overhead – small fry quite undone by the gangs of hooligan-shells that dash over to rend the German lines.' (At the corner of the page, he doodled what looks like a fatter, cartoon version of Munch's *Scream*.)

Under at least an attempt at a creeping barrage, the men of the 9th and 10th KOYLI, the 8th Somersets and the 4th Middlesex on the left flank advanced up the slope. The belt of conical explosions ahead of them, however, was too far, too thin and too brief. The machine-gunners in *König Trench* and *Red Cottage* were unaffected. With multiple weapons, they quartered the battlefield like segments of an orange, killing or wounding 800 men in less than ten minutes. The 4th Middlesex were hit so badly they had to withdraw before re-forming and advancing again as a single extended line. This time, at least, single bullets killed only one man at a time.

South of Tangier Trench, Second Lieutenant Howe advanced at the head of his men. Like a disciplined sprinter, he kept his eyes fixed on his objective. By the time he had crossed three deserted German lines and got to *Lonely Trench*, he allowed himself to turn round. He saw only a handful of breathless British soldiers and a subaltern wounded in the leg. The rest of the battalion was nowhere to be seen. Nor were the enemy – though a moment later a bewildered German rounded the traverse and shot Howe in the hand. On regaining consciousness and finding that his wound had been bandaged, Howe prepared to defend his hopelessly isolated position. The seriously wounded were placed in the heart of a dugout, the lightly so on the steps. The wounded subaltern stood at the top with a rifle, with Howe behind ready to reload.

At 7.45 a.m., Sassoon recorded 'I have seen the 21st Division advancing on the left of Fricourt; and some Huns apparently surrendering … Our men advancing steadily to the first line. A haze of smoke drifting across the landscape – brilliant sunshine. Some Yorkshires on our left watching the show and cheering as if at a football match.' The advancing members of the 21st Division were almost certainly the men of the KOYLI who, despite their losses, succeeded in overrunning the German front line. Those cheering were the '10 per cent' of the 10th West Yorks, ignorant of their comrades' fate.

The 1st East Yorks and the 15th Durham Light Infantry followed close behind the two Yorkshire battalions. Captain Rex Gee (DLI) recalled: 'Couldn't have faced it unless afraid of funking it before the men … awful havoc, terrible sights. Terrible slaughter by the Hun artillery and machine guns, the latter with snipers hurling bullets from every direction.' He reached the German lines: 'Had dozens of close

TAMBOURS

M. G.
F3a55.28 270 yds

Enemy Front Line
250 yds

Hare Lane
350 yds

Orchard Alley
1450 yds

Hidden Wood
F10b21.37 1900yds

Rabbit Lane
450 yds

Red Cottage
F3a81.60 480yds
M.G M.G M.G M.G.

FRICOURT

Sunshine Alley
1250yds

Red Trench
380yds

M.G

T

F3a56.15 270yds

shaves and admit to being in frightened stew throughout the whole advance. One Hun machine gunner held up his hands but … could not stop to secure him prisoner. As soon as first line passed over he turned his gun and mowed them down from behind … Makes you want to skin every Hun alive.'

By 8.00 a.m., elements of the KOYLI, DLI and East Yorkshires had made it to *Crucifix Trench*, a small victory blighted by news that men of the 11th Suffolks to their left had been burnt to death by a flame thrower. In the wake of this northern coalition's 1,200-yard advance lay the lifeless or crawling bodies of over 1,000 men of the 64th Brigade. Private Frank King was among them, wounded through the arm and lung. His brother Dick was not. As he moved across no man's land with a group of men from his platoon, an isolated German shell had fallen on top of them. The surviving soldiers waited for the smoke to clear, and then, finding no trace of their fellows, they carried on their march to the German lines.

The 64th Brigade's commander, Brigadier-General H. R. Headlam, had moved forward after his men to the *Sunken Lane*. Spurred by the death of Brigade Major G. B. Bosanquet while reconnoitring an assault to the side of Round Wood, General Headlam led the attack himself. A force combining men from six battalions followed, including Private J. G. Crossley of the 15th DLI: 'We were soon obliged to fall flat in the grass to escape the hail of machine-gun fire. As we lay there, a comrade beside me raised his head a little and asked me in which direction were the enemy lines … There was a sound like a plop, he gave a shudder and lay still. The bullet had passed through his eye. It was about this time that my feeling of confidence was replaced by an acceptance of the fact that I had been sent here to die.' Unsupported on either flank, General Headlam

ordered a halt to all further advances. Now reinforced by the 10th Green Howards and 1st Lincolns, he resolved to defend the ground gained for the rest of the day.

In their captured dugout in *Lonely Trench*, Second Lieutenant Howe's outpost of mostly wounded men had held back the Germans throughout the morning. With ammunition now running low, Howe asked his men whether they wished to make a fighting retreat or allow themselves to be taken prisoner. Agreement had just been reached that they would surrender with the final round when a party of soldiers from the 10th Yorks and Lancs appeared at the left-hand end of their position. The relieved men now made their way back through British-held trenches to their original lines.

Despite 50th Brigade's signal that any further efforts to advance were hopeless, Lieutenant-General Horne ordered the secondary attack to go ahead. Second Lieutenant Howe, now assuming command of his battalion as its only remaining officer, was invited to join in the assault. To the north of Fricourt, at 2.30 p.m. three companies of the 7th Green Howards and two companies of the 7th East Yorks, together with one wounded officer of the 10th West Yorks, went over. Sassoon watched the 20th Manchesters attack to the south: 'Could see about 400. Many walked casually across with sloped arms … Through my glasses I could see one man moving his arm up and down as he lay on his side; his face was a crimson patch. Others lay still in the sunlight.' A Private Pat Burke remembered the Manchesters' colonel uttering his last words as he mounted the ladder: 'Isn't it wonderful?' he said.

Within three minutes, the men advancing to the north of Fricourt village had suffered over 470 casualties. The survivors withdrew to the

British line. After a pause of only a few minutes, the CO of the Green Howards mustered the men for yet another effort. As he did so, he noticed another apparently able-bodied officer and approached him to join. Second Lieutenant Howe now faced his third trip of the day into no man's land. At the end of his endurance, Howe showed the Howards' CO his wounded hand and a hole in his cheek sustained during his second excursion. He was excused from taking part in the new attack.

On the evening of 2 July, Lieutenant-General Horne penned a letter to his wife: 'The artillery have done splendid work, the way we knocked about Mametz and Fricourt and the trenches round has been grand. All agree that the places were utterly demolished. My infantry fought splendidly, the old 7th Division in particular distinguished themselves … The 21st also did well north of Fricourt … All did splendid work and I did not have casualties as heavy as I expected to. The artillery covered the infantry advance so well. We are all very pleased with ourselves.'

Captain Rex Gee of the 15th DLI noted his own reflections in his diary the same day: 'Am dog-tired and not worth much. Everything was horrible, ghastly and awful. May I never experience the same again. Saw scores horribly wounded, horribly killed. Am being converted to conscientious objector. Cannot express the horrors of it all.'

* * *

Fricourt New Military Cemetery in Panorama ⓬ contains the graves of 210 British soldiers: 159 of them belong to men of the 10th West Yorkshire Regiment.

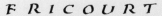

F R I C O U R T

Fricourt Wood

zig Trench
480 yds

Rose Trench
1300 yds

Ruins of Fricourt Church
F3a60.96 2000yds

The Orch
F4d35.90 13.

The Halt
F11a0.3 400 yds
M.G

Enemy Front Line
300 yds

British Front Line
Mansell Copse: 9th Devons
290 yds

Enemy Front Line
Danube Trench
430 yds

Hidden Lane
930 yds

Hidden Wood
F106.3.3 860 yds
M.G.

Tirpitz Trench
500 yds

Shrine Alley
640 yds

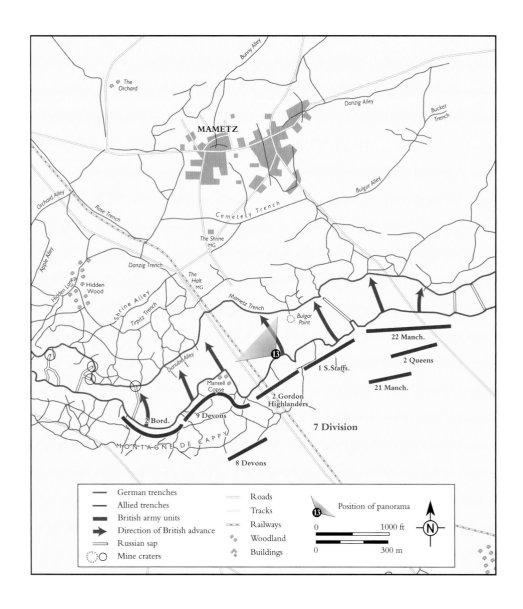

The Orchard

Bunny Alley

MAMETZ

Danzig Alley

Bucket Trench

Bulgar Alley

Orchard Alley

Rose Trench

Cemetery Trench

The Shrine MG

Apple Alley

Danzig Trench

The Halt MG

Mametz Trench

Bulgar Point

Hidden Wood

Hidden Lane

Shrine Alley

Tirpitz Trench

Danube Alley

13

22 Manch.

2 Queens

1 S.Staffs.

21 Manch.

Mansell Copse

2 Gordon Highlanders

2 Bord.

9 Devons

7 Division

MONTAGNE DE CAPPY

8 Devons

—— German trenches

—— Allied trenches

◼ British army units

➤ Direction of British advance

⊐ Russian sap

◯ Mine craters

┈ Roads

┈ Tracks

╫ Railways

Woodland

Buildings

Position of panorama

0   1000 ft

0   300 m

N

CHAPTER 9

MAMETZ

On 11 June 1916, the soldiers of the 9th Devonshire Regiment marched up to a section of the British front line in the open country between the villages of Mametz and Carnoy. Among them was a 23-year-old subaltern by the name of William Noel Hodgson, a veteran of a year's fighting, holder of the Military Cross and already a poet of some reputation. The great battle was coming, but for the next ten days the Devonshires' adopted trenches were peaceful.[1] In them, Lieutenant Hodgson would write the most affecting poem of the First World War.

Noel Hodgson was born in Thornley, Bristol, in 1893, but grew up in Northumberland, where his family had their roots. His clergyman father had accepted the coastal parish of Berwick-upon-Tweed, and Hodgson's childhood was spent in a house on Berwick's defensive sea wall. At twelve, he won a scholarship to Durham School, and five years later went up to Oxford, attending Christ Church as an exhibitioner. Awarded a first-class degree in Classical Moderations in March 1913 (the same month in which a poem of his first appeared in print), he decided to stay on and do 'Greats'. His studies, however, were cut short by the onset of war. Volunteering too late for the Border Regiment, he was granted a commission in the 9th Devons on 16 September 1914.

Under the command of Colonel Thomas A. H. Davies, a veteran of dusty Imperial soldiering, the battalion spent eleven months in training, first at Aldershot and then at Bordon Camp near Haslemere. On 27 July 1915, it travelled to France, initially manning the front line at Festubert. Hodgson was appointed bombing officer, seeing his first action on 25 September on the industrial wastelands of Loos, for which he received his MC, while 15 other officers and 461 men of the battalion were killed or wounded in the attack. February 1916 saw the Devonshires' arrival on the Somme battlefront. They spent the next four months manning positions mostly in front of Fricourt and then a line of trenches on the Montagne de Cappy, overlooking Mametz. It was to these trenches, in front of a small cluster of beech trees called Mansell Copse, that the battalion would return a week before the battle, and from which they would attack on 1 July.

The assault on Mametz was to be made by five battalions of the 7th Division (including the 9th Devons), with a further five battalions in support. Though now added to by New Army units (the Devonshire and Manchester battalions), the 7th Division was a Regular Army formation. Six regular battalions would take part in the attack. After two weeks of 'careful and systematic' rehearsals, the 7th Division men were 'thoroughly prepared for battle'. The Germans at Mametz, however, were not.

---

1 The position from which Panorama ⓭ was taken.

3 made at *c7.30am. BST* on *c1st July 2015* from *NW of Stafford St: 2nd Gordon Highlanders 7.30am. BST 1st July 1916*

including a field view of *99°* from about *N* to *WSW*

Approximate Scale of Degrees (1 degree equals *½* inches).

| 2 | 3 | 4 | 5 | 6 | 7 | 8 | 9 | 10 | 11 | 12 |

MAMETZ

Bulgar Point
F11b25.18 240yds

Bunny Wood
F5a25.61 1460yds

Ruins of Mametz Church
F5c50.45 960yds

lley
ds

Willow Stream
1600yds

FO

Pa

O

The Shrine
11a 29.65 580 yds
M.G.

Cemetery Trench
580 yds

Orchard Trench
900 yds

Enemy Front Line
Mametz Trench

M.G.
F5c 25.15 840yds

240 yds

M.G.
F11a 79.81 630 yds

Reserve Infanterie Regiment 109 had arrived from Ovillers on 16 June to find the defences around the village far inferior to those they had left. There were not enough dugouts to accommodate the trench garrison, and the few that existed were almost all positioned inside the front line. The main lines of trenches (also too few) were not adequately protected by wire, and there was a shortage of communication trenches to reach them by. The Bavarian Pioniers worked night and day to remedy these deficiencies, but by the start of the British bombardment on 24 June the job was far from done.

The relative weakness of the enemy positions was, however, far from clear to the British soldiers facing them, least of all to a captain and friend of Hodgson's in the 9th Devonshires, whose name would become part of the folklore of the battle.

Duncan Lenox Martin features in even the shortest accounts of 1 July, yet he remains an enigmatic figure. Details of his life before the war are scarce. Born in Algiers in May 1886, he appears to have spent his childhood in Hailsham in Sussex, although in 1891 his father described himself as an ostrich farmer in the Cape Colony. Apart from a German governess, the only record of Martin's education is as a fifteen-year-old boarder at the Channel View School in Walton in Gordano in Somerset. He travelled to Germany with his mother and sister in 1903, but no further record of his life exists before he applied for his commission on 9 September 1914. Different sources describe him as an artist or a maths teacher. One private soldier in his battalion intriguingly referred to him as 'the secret service man'.[2] Whatever the case, it was as a model maker that he would make his mark on history.

While on leave in the second week of June, Martin made a plasticine replica of the Mametz battlefield. From it, he deduced that there was likely to be a dense concentration of machine-gun fire across the ground that the 9th Devons were scheduled to advance over. On his return to France, he shared his creation with 20th Brigade HQ. The commonly told story has it that Martin's theory was summarily dismissed by his superiors, but in fact, as Charlotte Zeepvat has revealed in her 2015 biography of Noel Hodgson, *Before Action*, they gave orders for the model to be inspected by every officer in the division. Indeed, the overview afforded by Martin's structure led commanders to adjust minor details of the attack. The overall plan and timings, however, remained unchanged. The assaults of the leading five battalions, including that of the 9th Devons through Mansell Copse, were to go ahead at zero hour as scheduled.

On 30 June, the 9th Devons rested in the Bois des Tailles. The 8th Battalion chaplain, the Rev. Ernest Crosse, gave communion. In the evening, the battalion's 22 officers made a bonfire and sang before marching their 753 men up to the front at 10.30 p.m. As the front line had been damaged by shelling, they formed up in reserve trenches that offered greater protection from any German barrage. The men would,

---

2 While there appears to be no direct evidence that Martin was a member of the nascent MI6, it is certainly a strange remark for a fellow soldier (particularly a private) to make out of the blue. The fact that the character witnesses on his application for a commission were two high-ranking officers including Colonel Davies (when Martin himself had no previous military record or qualification) prompts further speculation still. Davies also attested in the application to Martin having 'very good French and German'. A note in red ink, furthermore, was added to the form: 'This gentleman explains his late application by his difficulty in returning home from France where he was when war broke out.' Even his nickname, given by fellow officers, must be said to carry a hint of duplicity, even of a codename: 'Iscariot'.

however, have to advance a further 250 yards in the attack. They would now leave their trenches three minutes early to cover the extra distance.

At 6.25 a.m., Noel Hodgson and Duncan Martin watched as the bombardment of Mametz intensified. They then sat on the fire step and ate sandwiches. Second Lieutenant Rowan Freeland was with them: 'We were all very cheery and I don't hesitate in saying that dear old "Uncle"[3] was the cheeriest of the lot.' Hodgson would go forward with his section of Welsh bombers in the second wave. His batman, Alfred Frederick Weston (alias 'Pearson'), to whom Hodgson was devoted, would go with them[4]. As the minutes ticked away, the officers in the first wave, including Captain Martin and Second Lieutenant Freeland, informed the waiting men of their early departure. With the barrage still raging overhead, they gave the scarcely audible instruction to fix bayonets. At 7.27 a.m. exactly, they went over.

Three minutes later, the advancing figures of the 9th Devons and 2nd Borders were joined by the leading men of the battalions to the east of the Albert–Carnoy Road. Unteroffizier Paul Scheytt of RIR 109 was watching: 'The English came walking, as though they were going to the theatre … We felt they were mad. Our orders were given in complete calm and every man took careful aim to avoid wasting ammunition.'

By 7.45 a.m., assisted by the detonation of two mines at *Bulgar Point*, the leading men of the 1st South Staffs had passed through the German front line and were advancing on the southern outskirts of Mametz. By 8.30 a.m., the Manchesters had reached *Bucket Trench*, though not before Unteroffizier Scheytt and his fellow machine-gunners in *Cemetery Trench* had taken a heavy toll. 'We'd just topped a little fold in the ground, when we walked straight into a zone of machine-gun fire,' recorded a 'gentleman sergeant' of the 22nd Manchesters, Richard Henry (Harry) Tawney. 'The whole line dropped like one man, some dead and wounded, the rest taking instinctively to such cover as the ground offered.' Raising himself to his knees to wave the cowering body of men forward, Tawney was shot through the chest and abdomen.

On the left flank of the assault, the 2nd Borders too had suffered heavy losses from machine-gunners in Fricourt and Mametz as well as enfilade fire from *Hidden Wood*. Combining a bombing raid down *Hidden Lane* with an attack across the open, however, the Borderers succeeded in overrunning the *Hidden Wood* position. Their marksmanship impressed Grenadier Emil Kury: 'There were five of us on our machine gun when I saw an English soldier about twenty metres away on our left. Then our oldest soldier, a painter who came from Pforzheim and had five children, was shot in the forehead … Next I was shot in the chest. I felt the blood run down my back and I fell … He shot three of us before I had chance to use my rifle. I would like to meet that English soldier. He was a good shot.' By 10.00 a.m., the Borderers had secured their objective of *Apple Alley*.

---

3 Hodgson's sister Stella had given birth to her first child (his goddaughter) on 16 June, his pride at which clearly attracted the nickname. He was more usually known by his brother officers as 'Smiler'.

4 Hodgson had written a sketch of 'Pearson' in *The New Witness* (a weekly newspaper founded as *The Eye-Witness* by Hilaire Belloc in 1911 and edited by G. K. Chesterton from 1916 to 1923): 'He is my servant, and if he were Commander-in-Chief the war would be over in a week. But I would get no baths, so I'm glad he isn't. "Pearson" can manage anything. There are many like him, I am sure, but I prefer to think of him as supreme.'

Further down the hill to their right, however, there was as yet no sign of British khaki. The German machine-gun positions at *The Shrine* and to the west of the village had survived the British bombardment. In the three minutes before zero hour, they had killed or wounded two 9th Devonshire soldiers every second. Marching 'in perfect order' through Captain Martin's predicted concentration of fire, most of the Devons were hit before reaching the British front line, but small groups did make it through the front German defences. Reinforced through the morning by a costly 8th Battalion advance, they consolidated a position in *Tirpitz Trench* by 2.30 p.m.

Across the road to the east, the 2nd Gordon Highlanders were initially held up by uncut wire in front of the German positions. Facing close-range machine-gun fire, they fought their way to *Shrine Alley* before being pinned down, along with the South Staffs and Manchesters to their right, on the edge of Mametz. Following a further bombardment of the German positions at 3.30 p.m., men from five battalions resumed their efforts to capture the village. Private J. Kirkham of the Manchester Pals recalled a typical brutal encounter: 'I was just about to jump into a German trench when a Jerry made a lunge at me with his bayonet … but just took a small piece out of my thigh. Instead of a rifle, I had a knobkerrie … I hit out at him and sank it deep into his forehead … His helmet came off and I saw that he was a bald-headed old man. I have never forgotten that bald head and I don't suppose I ever will.'

Now threatened with the loss of the village, the German garrison fought with desperate courage. At the end of the battle, only 32 of the more than 2,100 men of RIR 109 made it back to their second line. The only surviving gun of Feldartillerie-Regiment 29 fired 2,300 rounds throughout the day before becoming unserviceable. Hauptmann Fröhlich emptied his wine cellars to reward his tireless men. One by one, machine-gun positions were outflanked by advancing British soldiers or strafed by RFC aircraft, and front-line supplies of ammunition were almost exhausted. The defenders had had little or no water for 24 hours. One of Unteroffizier Scheytt's men 'went completely mad from thirst. He was foaming at the mouth and, despite our shouts, ran blindly out of our trench … and was shot down.' By 4.05 p.m., the village was in British hands.

The capture of Mametz marked one of only two achieved British objectives on 1 July. A Private H. L. Wilde of the 9th Devons, both victorious and alive, reflected: 'The sun went down that first evening back over our old trenches, in gold which turned to blood, and it seemed symbolic. We had kept our nerve and at the end of the day we were where we were supposed to be and that seemed triumph enough to be going on with.'

Unlike other sectors, here the British advance allowed medics and stretcher-bearers a proper chance to recover the wounded. For some men, a lethal dose of morphine was the most that could be offered. Others were luckier. Sergeant Tawney had lain apparently mortally wounded on the battlefield for twelve hours. He was now attended by 'an angel', a corporal of the Royal Army Medical Corps. 'It was a lovely evening, and a man stood beside me. I caught him by the ankle, in terror lest he should vanish … He can't have been more than twenty-six or twenty-seven; but his face seemed to shine with love and comprehension … I was like a dog kicked and bullied by everyone that's at last found a kind master, and in a grovelling kind of way I worshipped him.'[5]

The Rev. Ernest Crosse likewise returned to the battlefield on an errand of mercy. He had gone over with the 8th Devons earlier that day. Defying the wishes of the battalion commander, at 3.30 p.m. he accompanied a medical officer to the back of Mansell Copse. 'The road was strewn with dead,' he remembered, 'almost the first I looked at being Martin.' One of Hodgson's bombers, a Private Jack Owen, was witness to the moment Martin went down: 'He had gone 15 yards when he was shot through the head above the right temple. He turned his head to the left, flung out his right arm and fell dead on his back.' As well as Martin, the 9th Devons suffered sixteen other officer casualties that day, including Noel Hodgson.

There are two versions of Hodgson's fate, but the true one is clear. Ernest Crosse found Hodgson's body a hundred yards from Martin's, on the rise before Mansell's Copse. He had been hit in the leg by a machine-gun round then killed by another through the neck after he fell. Pearson lay alongside him. In the batman's hand was an unwrapped bandage.

On 26 June, Hodgson had written his final letter to his sister, a short, conversational note signed off with 'Haven't time for more at present.' But he had already sent home another envelope, and the message inside was not private but open, addressed to anyone that cared to read it: the pencilled lines he had written in the trenches overlooking the hill where he was killed.

I, that on my familiar hill
Saw with uncomprehending eyes
A hundred of thy sunsets spill
Their fresh and sanguine sacrifice,
Ere the sun swings his noonday sword
Must say good-bye to all of this; –
By all delights that I shall miss,
Help me to die, O Lord.[6]

---

5 R. H. Tawney (1880–1962) became a leading economist and Christian Socialist and a key figure in the Labour movement. A. L. Rowse (1903–97) maintained that 'Tawney exercised the widest influence of any historian of his time, politically, socially and, above all, educationally.'

6 The final stanza of 'Before Action', first published in *The New Witness* on 29 June 1916, the date for which the attack was originally scheduled. It is commonly understood that the 'familiar hill' that Hodgson had in mind is that of Durham School, to the west of the cathedral.

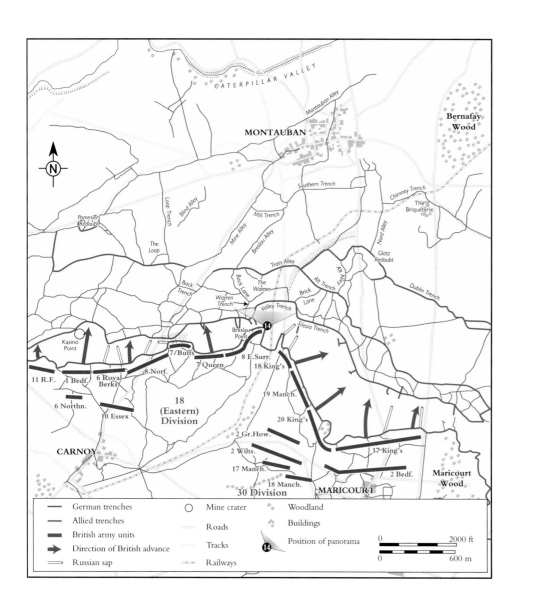

CATERPILLAR VALLEY

Montauban Alley

MONTAUBAN

Bernafay
Wood

Southern Trench

Chimney Trench

Loop Trench

Blind Alley

Mill Trench

The
Briqueterie

Pommiers
Redoubt

Mine Alley

Breslau Alley

Nord Alley

Glatz
Redoubt

The
Loop

Train Alley

Back
Trench

Back Lane

The
Warren

Alt Trench

Alt Alley

Dublin Trench

Warren
Trench

Brick
Lane

Valley Trench

Silesia Trench

Breslau
Point

14

Kasino
Point

7/Buffs

8 E.Surr.

11 R.F.

1 Bedf.

6 Royal
Berks.

8.Norf.

7 Queen

18 King's

6 Northn.

10 Essex

18
(Eastern)
Division

19 Manch.

20 King's

2 Gr.How.

17 King's

CARNOY

2 Wilts.

17 Manch.

2 Bedf.

18 Manch.

Maricourt
Wood

30 Division

MARICOURT

——	German trenches	○	Mine crater
——	Allied trenches		
▬▬	British army units		Roads
➤	Direction of British advance		Tracks
≡	Russian sap		Railways

Woodland

Buildings

Position of panorama

14

0   2000 ft

0   600 m

CHAPTER 10

MONTAUBAN

On the evening of 29 April 2015, the National Trust's Palladian mansion of Clandon Park in Surrey was burnt to a shell. The fire destroyed the glory of Giacomo Leoni's great marble hall, commissioned by Lord Onslow in the 1730s, together with a priceless collection of treasures curated over three centuries. It was the greatest heritage disaster in the trust's 120-year history. Yet the loss that many felt most deeply, and that headlined the blaze in many newspapers, was not of a piece of Meissen porcelain or rare sculpted stucco but of a 1916 stitched leather football by A. W. Gamage Ltd of High Holborn, London. Purchased by 21-year-old Captain Wilfred 'Billie' Nevill on his last leave before the great Somme offensive, it was one of two that had returned with him to the trenches. On the morning of 1 July, two platoons of the 8th East Surreys kicked them all the way to the village of Montauban.

The 1,600-yard journey of Captain Nevill's footballs[1] (though not of Captain Nevill himself) marked the British army's headiest achievement during the Somme's first day. If the British had chosen to attack nowhere else, the battle might still be remembered as one of the great national victories of the war. With the French on their right flank, eleven battalions of the 18th and 30th divisions led the advance northwards over the open country to the east of Mametz. By 11.00 a.m., they had taken Montauban and glimpsed the view across an unscarred valley to Longueval, 'where the trees had leaves and even the air seemed sweeter'. That night, many victorious British soldiers thought the war was as good as over.

Not all those who had taken part felt equally triumphant, however. Although unaware of the battles lost further to the north, many survivors of this southernmost assault found a battle won hard to distinguish. Nearly 4,000 of them had sustained some sort of injury. Those able to walk had retired half-bandaged from the battlefield throughout the day 'like a crowd leaving a football match' to the advance dressing station at Minden Post.[2] Others, more seriously injured but judged possible to save, were laid in the heat of Carnoy village square. Some bled to death on the cobbles. In General Rawlinson's diary entry that evening, the advance of XIII Corps was the brightest consoling light in an otherwise almost hopeless battlefield. Yet moving forwards to success had proved only fractionally less costly than wholesale retreat. The troops committed

---

1 Both balls were inscribed by Nevill. On one he wrote: 'The Great European Cup-Tie Final. East Surreys v. Bavarians. Kick off at zero.' On the other: 'No referee.' A prize was offered to the platoon whose ball first made it to their objective, but Nevill was not able to present the award. He was killed in the opening moments of the attack just short of *Valley Trench*.

2 In the process, some became unwitting film stars. The cameraman John Benjamin MacDowell had spent the afternoon at Minden Post selectively filming the treatment of the wounded for the summer's great theatrical presentation.

t Line

Warren Trench
300 yds

Mill Trench
1000 yds

The Warren
A3c 42.10 320 yds
M.G

Valley Trench
250 yds

Train Alley
320 yds

Montauban Alley
1800 yds

Pommiers Redoubt
A36.3 1700 yds
M.G s

M.G.
A86 95.77 280 yds

Breslau Point
A9a 35.70 200 yds

The Loop
A2c 79.80 1150 yds
M.G

Loop Trench
1250 yds

Back Trench
850 yds

M.G
A2d 16.29 850 yds

Blind Alley
1150 yds

Back Lane
430 yds

Enem

Mine Alley
860 yds

to the battle for Montauban represented 14 per cent of the total British attacking force. Their losses still amounted to over 10 per cent of the whole: a total of 6,126 men.

Since the initial deadlock in the autumn of 1914, the lines between Mametz and Curlu had been the quietest on the Somme sector. There had been the occasional raid to keep up appearances, and the Germans had dug a mine under the French in the spring of 1915, but generally the opposing sides had existed in a state of uncertain yet strangely pastoral calm, more uncharitable thoughts being swapped between them than actual shells. The local French farmers had continued to grow and gather what crops they could and to sell their produce to both sides, frustrating military convoys with their huge-wheeled carts. It seems that the Somme's wildlife benefited too from this local air of détente: the accounts of British soldiers contain more references to their natural neighbours here than anywhere else on the battlefront. A private in the 7th Bedfords recalled rescuing a covey of English partridge chicks from a trench sump on the eve of the battle and watching with satisfaction as the hen bird 'chuckled them off, never to be seen again'. Advancing soldiers at zero hour flushed a number of hares from the grasses in front of the German positions. When the 16th and 17th Manchesters occupied the wreckage of Montauban later that morning, they found the only thing living was a fox.

The German defences here too were lackadaisical. While the wiring and earthworks at Mametz were sub-standard, at Montauban they had been constructed carelessly. The Upper Silesian defenders were unconcerned, however. They had been assured that the French were capable of nothing more than sustaining their bloody defence of Verdun.

The assembly of British battalions alongside them was simply a feint to hold their attention. When the British and French artillery unleashed their firestorm on 25 June, the German garrison cursed their own intelligence officers as profanely as they did the allied gunners. The week-long preliminary bombardment would be more punishing at Montauban than anywhere else on the fifteen-mile front.

Whereas only 14 heavy batteries protected the German positions, the British and French had 50. Heavy howitzers were placed at 47-yard intervals along the allied front, with a field gun every 17 yards. On their way to Agincourt, Henry's soldiers had razed the small hamlet of Montauban with hand-held torches. The British guns now obliterated its 247 houses at a range of three miles. By 27 June, the village was a ruin. The weakest of the German shelters had been smashed like sandcastles. Desperate German defenders migrated from dugout to dugout until the more robust defences could admit no more of them. Nor were the German gunners spared. Twelve allied batteries, more than in any other sector, were allocated to counter-battery fire. By 11.00 a.m. on the morning of the attack, the German artillery was virtually silenced.

For the first three hours of daylight on 1 July, the ground in front of Montauban was shrouded in thick eddies of low white cloud. At 6.25 a.m., with observation still impossible, the combined might of 300 British and French guns accelerated to a 'hurricane' rate of fire. Lieutenant G. Chetwynd-Stapleton of 9 Squadron RFC was flying overhead. 'It was like looking at a large lake of mist, with thousands of stones being thrown into it,' he recalled later. The 'stones' were 4.7- to 15-inch calibre shells which fell through the mist at a rate of nearly 1,000 rounds a minute. It was the greatest concentration of shellfire of the day.

Fold out for Panorama 14: *Montauban*

Its final climax, like a flourish on a bass drum, left a silence as concussive as the explosions. At 7.25 a.m., British and French soldiers mounted their scaling ladders and formed up in no man's land. At 7.30, the flag fell and, *coude à coude* (Colonel Fairfax, commander of the 1st Liverpool Pals, and Commandant Le Petit of the French 153 RI linked arms), they were off.

On the plains north of Maricourt, the Liverpool Pals of 89 Brigade moved forward. For most, it was their first action. With slung rifles, almost every soldier smoked as they advanced, tight-lipped through pincered fingers. They need not have worried. By 8.30 a.m., they had taken their objective of *Dublin Trench* at a cost of only 24 casualties. The 17th Kings lost not a single man killed. 'It all seemed so easy,' Lance Corporal Quinn of the 20th Kings wrote home afterwards, 'much easier than when we had practised it behind the line.' Even 89 Brigade's commander could scarcely credit the rate of the advance. As if witnessing his own horse leading round Tattenham Corner, Brigadier-General The Hon. F. C. Stanley[3] now left the grandstand and made his way onto the course. 'I can see him now,' recalled Sergeant Ernest Bryan of the 17th Kings; 'he was up within our front line within an hour and a half of our taking it. Not standing in a trench but standing in the open with a pair of field glasses.' His view improved further. By midday, his men were in the Briqueterie. The German defenders were taken prisoner in their bare feet.

On the left flank of the assault, the greatest initial threat to the 1st Bedfords, 6th Berkshires and 8th Norfolks was not German but British. On 30 June, British tunnellers had placed a 5,000 lb mine under the German stronghold of *Casino Point*. Now, at zero hour, an officer of the Royal Engineers faced an invidious dilemma. As he placed his palm on the plunger, the leading British troops were already approaching the charge. In a decision made, one imagines, less by his brain than by his fingers, the officer blew the mine. By a utilitarian calculation at least, he chose correctly. Although flying debris the size of suitcases brutally disfigured many British soldiers, the Germans' frontal resistance now dissolved. British soldiers pressed on to *Pommiers Redoubt*, where the German defenders were still unwilling to concede. In a manoeuvre that sidestepped British tactical orthodoxy as well as the enemy positions, a small group of Norfolks advanced past the east flank of the strongpoint and brought enfilade fire down on the defenders. By 8.45 a.m., the British had taken the redoubt.

In the centre, progress was slower. Bearing testament to the resilience of human flesh under shellfire, the British advance was checked by no fewer than eight machine-gunners still able to man their weapons. Emplacements in *Train Alley* and at the junction of *Alt Trench* and *Alt Alley* (MG A3d70.19) killed or wounded over a thousand soldiers of the lead battalions (including Captain Nevill) in under an hour before being knocked out by heroic solo bombing actions. But the defensive line was disordered. Remaining strongpoints could be outflanked. Although some diehard gunners held out (one, at *Breslau Point*, was found chained to his weapon), soon British numbers, supported by the machine guns of British aircraft, overran all German second-line trenches. By 8.45 a.m., *Glatz Redoubt* had fallen into British hands.

---

3 Brother of the 17th Earl of Derby whose 1914 recruitment campaign had raised the Liverpool battalions.

4 made at c.7.30 a.m. BST on c.1st July 2015 from W of Talus Boise : 8th East Surreys 7.30 a.m. BST 1st July 1916

including a field view of 122° from about WNW to ENE

Approximate Scale of Degrees (1 degree equals 2/5 inches).

2   3   4   5   6   7   8   9   10   11   12

Silesia Trench

Alt Trench
650 yds   300 yds

M.G.
A3d 70.19 650 yds

Brick Lane
580 yds   Dublin Trench
GLATZ REDOUBT   1260 yds
A4c3.6 1260 yds
M.G.

Chimney Trench   The Briqueterie
1550 yds   A4b3.4 1700 yds

1. Panoramas are taken solely for military purposes.
2. The publication of them in the press will necessarily give valuable information to the enemy.
3. This panorama is to be kept with as much security as is compatible with full advantage of it being taken by our own troops.
4. When troops are relieved this panorama should be handed over to the relieving troops.

ONTAUBAN

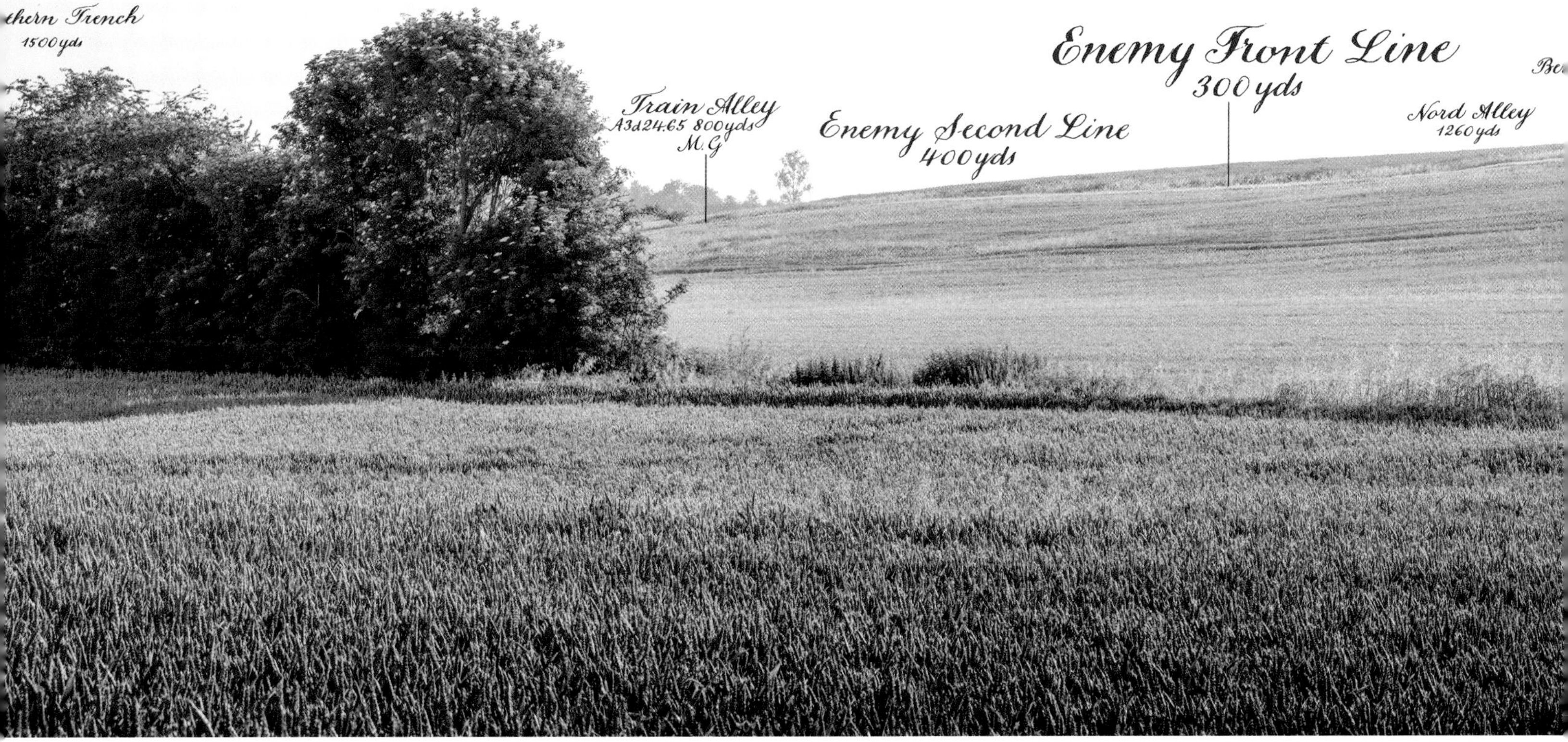
thern Trench
1500 yds
Train Alley
A3d24.65 800yds
M.G
Enemy Second Line
400yds
Enemy Front Line
300 yds
Nord Alley
1260yds

Isolated pockets of resistance were now 'mopped up'. Private W. C. Bennett and his fellow Norfolks discovered a way to save their Mills bombs: 'In clearing the dugouts that usually had two entrances, we first of all shouted for the occupants to come out. If this had no effect, we would throw a heavy stone down one entrance which would generally send them all racing out the other end.' Private Jack Cousins of the 7th Bedfords was less frugal: 'We came to a Jerry dugout. I pulled the pin of a Mills bomb and threw it down. There was a bit of a bang after four seconds, then I heard someone moaning. I went down into the dugout, and there was this Jerry laid with a great hole in his chest, blood pouring everywhere, pointing to his mouth. I gave him my water bottle. The water went in his mouth, and came out of the holes. He was gone in a few seconds.' One 7th Queens officer despatched the hapless defenders like a cowboy in a western saloon: 'Our platoon commander had a mouth of the dugout on either side of him, say 15 yards away. A German would rush out of No. 1 exit – over he went. Then one would come out of No.2 exit, and over he went. Our officer was as cool as a cucumber … It was the best bit of fancy shooting I've seen – all prizes, no blanks.'

As the still ordered lines of British soldiers reached Montauban, they met a scene of grim devastation. There were 'bodies everywhere, in all kinds of attitudes, some on fire and burning from the British bombardment. Debris and deserted equipment littered the area and papers were fluttering around in the breeze.'[4] Pressing on to Montauban Alley in the late afternoon, they witnessed the last tattered remnants of the enemy garrison sprinting across Caterpillar Valley to the German second line. General Congreve wanted to follow them. Shortly after 5 p.m., he telephoned Rawlinson for permission to continue the advance. The 4th Army commander received the call in the drawing room of his headquarters at Querrieux. His orders from Haig were clear: 'Opportunities to use cavalry, supported by guns, machine-guns etc. and infantry should be sought for, both during the early stages of the attack and subsequently.' The German second positions to the north were now manned by cooks, orderlies, clerks and servants. Patrols had confirmed Bernafay and Trones Woods to the east were deserted, beyond which triumphant French soldiers were straining at the leash. Congreve had one fresh infantry division and the 2nd Indian Cavalry Division in reserve, and five more hours of daylight. Yet Rawlinson refused to let him move. The plan had made no provision for a breakthrough in the south. Congreve's men were to stay put. By midnight, the gap in the German line had healed. The bloody fighting to capture it over the following weeks would cost the lives of thousands more British soldiers, including Congreve's own son.[5]

For their part, the conquering heroes of the 18th and 30th divisions were content to enjoy their gains. In between consolidating their defences, many ordinary soldiers devoted the evening to souvenir hunting, a German *Pickelhaube* helmet being the most sought-after prize. The nine remaining officers of the 8th East Surreys shared a bottle of champagne labelled 'To be drunk in Montauban "on der Tag"', and in the 10th Essex's newly acquired HQ in *Mine Alley* a table was laid for a bully beef dinner in celebration.

---

4 In the aftermath of battle, surviving soldiers (of both sides) would frequently search corpses for valuables or souvenirs. The personal letters, postcards and photographs found in the pockets of dead men were invariably discarded.

5 Major William 'Billy' La Touche Congreve, VC, DSO, MC (1891–1916) was killed by a sniper at Longueval on 20 July. He and his father are one of three father-and-son pairings to be awarded the Victoria Cross.

Brigadier-General H. W. Higginson, commander of 53 Brigade, joined them for whisky, chocolate and German cigars. Together they toasted the great British victory on the Somme.

* * *

Further north, fewer glasses were being raised. Most available tables were disinfected and sweated over by medics in vests and bloody aprons. Others were 'piled high with amputated limbs'. As a heavy dusk closed in, thick with the dust and fumes of the battle, stretcher-bearers worked through the darkness. Some bearers' hands were so scarred and blistered that they carried their loads using slings around their necks. In tented theatres, doctors and surgeons dabbed, bound, cut and injected their patients, while in the moribund wards (for those with no hope of survival), young men politely asked nurses if they were going to die. In the depths of no man's land near the German positions, the wounded who could not be brought in crawled into shell holes and waited. Many 'wrapped their waterproof groundsheets around them, took out their Bibles and died like that'.

From Gommecourt to Montauban, the night sky still flickered here and there with yellow gun flashes. The odd shell whined through the chilly air like an out-of-season firework. As 1 July drew to an end, the rattle of machine guns could still be heard now and then at Fricourt, Ovillers and the shoulder of Thiepval. Single rifle shots cracked in protest at the growing silence. In the minutes before midnight, two platoons of the 7th Lincolns crept out to the German lines north of Gommecourt, where a group of Sherwood Foresters was believed to be still holding out. The Lincolns found no surviving British soldiers, only a sky bright with Very lights and heavy German rifle fire. Just 42 out of 80 men made it back to the British line. It was the very last action of the day.

At the 10th Essex HQ in *Mine Alley*, only the adjutant, a Second Lieutenant Randolph Chell, took no part in the festivities. He sat in one corner on the telephone to Brigade. He made his report of the battalion's successes and asked for any news from elsewhere. The response he could make out jarred with the smell of Scotch and cigar smoke: the attacks to the north had failed at an estimated cost of 16,000 casualties.

Yet for now, Chell and the British High Command knew only the quarter of it. It would take staff officers a week of grim mathematics to establish the unheralded truth. It would take burial parties in gloves and facemasks more than eight months to verify the full details. Out of a total of 116,000 British and Empire soldiers committed to the battle over the course of the day, 57,470 had become casualties. 19,240 of them were dead.

AFTERMATH

The following morning, the lights in the house of Madame de la Rochefoucauld in Amiens were on well before dawn. Six correspondents of the British press, dressed in officer's uniform, were poised over their typewriters. They had watched the previous day's events from a rise on the Amiens road a mile behind Albert. Yet their grandstand view had revealed nothing of the truth of the battle. Nor would their copy. Just after 2 a.m., a messenger had arrived with the morning's communiqué from Haig's headquarters. Now, under the scrutiny of army censors, the newspapermen set down the world's first reports of the greatest offensive in history: 'Everything has gone well,' wrote H. P. Robinson of *The Times* under the headline of FORWARD IN THE WEST. 'Our troops have successfully carried out their missions ... large numbers of prisoners have been taken. Thanks to the very complete and effective artillery preparation, thanks also to the dash of our infantry, our losses have been very slight ... The first impression is that our leaders in the field are ... directing a methodical and well-planned advance.'

General Haig's personal diary entry on the evening of 1 July was similarly sparing of the reality: 'On a 16 mile front of attack varying fortune must be expected! ... The enemy are still in Fricourt, but we are round his flank on the north and close to Contalmaison. Ovillers and Thiepval villages have held our troops up, but our men are in the Schwaben Redoubt ... the VIII Corps said they began well, but as the day progressed their troops were forced back into the German front line, except two battalions which occupied Serre village and were it is said cut off. I am inclined to believe from further reports that few of the VIII Corps left their trenches!'[1] On the following morning, Sunday 2 July, after attending the Church of Scotland service in St Omer, Haig was informed by the adjutant-general that the total casualties for the previous day were now estimated at 40,000. 'This cannot be considered severe,' he recorded, with an even greater eye on history, 'in view of the numbers engaged, and the length of front attacked.'

---

1 This remark (in any case ill judged – though Haig made no effort subsequently to expunge it from the record) illustrates more starkly than any other the degree to which communication broke down during (and after) the battle. The infantry of 1 July were fated to attack not only without the support of tanks and co-ordinated aerial support but also crucially without portable radios. 'Walkie-talkies' did not exist in the First World War. As the historian John Terraine has commented: 'One hundred and fifty of them on [the first day of] the Somme might have made all the difference.'

2 VIII Corps comprised the 4th, 29th, 31st and 49th divisions.

While Haig sat over his diary on the evening of 1 July, 14,591 of the VIII Corps men that 'had not left their trenches' were lying dead or wounded in front of Serre and Beaumont Hamel.[2] From in front of the four 'gospel copses', recorded Unteroffizier Otto Lais, 'came one great moan'. Here and along the whole front, the task of recovering the human wreckage of the battle went on. In places the enemy permitted the collection of British wounded to be carried out in safety. At Gommecourt and Serre, redundant German first-aiders left their own trenches to assist in the effort, some erstwhile defenders taking one end of British stretchers. At Beaumont Hamel, a German officer himself raised a white flag while his own men carried injured British soldiers back to German lines. (When British brigade headquarters heard that these acts of mercy included the retrieval of abandoned British weapons, they ordered their front-line troops to fire on the German stretcher bearers. The British soldiers were unwilling to comply.) For most of the recovering German garrisons, however, the memory of the British bombardment prevented such humane concessions, and most attempts by British soldiers to rescue their stricken comrades were made under German fire. Despite widespread acts of individual heroism,[3] most of those left bleeding on the battlefield would stay and die where they were, some keeping a diary of their final hours and days.[4] A number were revived by a heavy downpour on the afternoon on 2 July and could be seen crawling, in agonised stages, back towards the British lines. Others, too damaged to move, were drowned by the rising water in the trenches or shell holes where they lay.

For several days, both officers and men braved no man's land in search of the living; the dead were left where they fell. For weeks and months afterwards, British sentries would look out on the silhouettes of British corpses slowly disintegrating on the German wire. Only those whose bodies lay behind or mere yards in front of the British front line could be gathered up without undue risk of further casualties. Save for the odd gently-spoken instruction, the work was carried out in silence. Many of the dead were lifted from the battlefield by their friends. Newly-arrived reserves shared the burden in awe of both the dead and the 'stary, rabbit-eyed' survivors they toiled alongside. Supervised by battalion padres (a number of whom had followed their communicants into battle), all recognisably intact bodies were laid in neat rows, and their identity discs collected where possible.[5] Already fly-blown, the dead were buried either as soon as graves could be dug or in existing trenches,

---

3 Two of the nine '1 July' Victoria Crosses were awarded for bringing in wounded under fire in the aftermath of the battle, to Rifleman Robert Quigg of the 12th Royal Irish Rifles, and posthumously to Lieutenant Geoffrey St George Shillington Cather of the 9th Royal Irish Fusiliers. Before the war, Rifleman Quigg had worked on the MacNaghten estate at Bushmills in County Antrim. Having joined up in 1914, he became batman to Second Lieutenant Sir Harry MacNaghten, the 6th Baronet. On hearing on the morning of 2 July that MacNaghten was missing, Quigg ventured out into no man's land seven times to search for him, each time bringing back another wounded man from the battlefield. MacNaghten was never found, however. On his death, the baronetcy transferred to his brother Douglas, serving with the Rifle Brigade. Douglas was killed near Delville Wood on the Somme ten weeks later. Rifleman Quigg died in 1955.

4 There were some remarkable stories of survival, however. Soldiers continued to struggle back to the British lines for up to a week, including a lieutenant from the 7th Sherwood Foresters who was hit seven times along the way. The record belongs to a private of the 4th London who was recovered in no man's land 14 days after the battle. Stuck in the mud, his wounds had not gone septic and he recovered after a year in hospital.

5 Soldiers wore two identity discs: one green, one red. In the event of their death, the green disc was collected to inform casualty lists; the red disc was left around the neck to identify the body to the burial party.

in which some had waited during their final hours. (On 4 July, Chaplain Crosse buried 163 Devons, including Duncan Martin and Noel Hodgson, in a trench – named Blood Alley – behind Mansell Copse alongside where they died.) Short funeral services were held in intervals between the shelling, and wooden crosses, fashioned from duckboards or trench timber and inscribed in lead paint, often with multiple names, were erected over the ground. Padres then wrote to the homes of the fallen with the consolation that their boy had been buried in the sight of God. Letters from young subalterns followed. In time, nearly 20,000 families would read handwritten details of a brave and faithful soldier and a noble, instantaneous death.

For days following the battle, however, the British people remained ignorant of the fate of their young men. High-flown headlines of 'heroic advances' and 'enemy trenches occupied' persisted in national newspapers through the first week of July. But soon the raw figures were impossible to camouflage. In any case, eye-witnesses of the battle were arriving home in their thousands. From midday on Sunday, ships packed with the wounded sailed for Southampton from Rouen, Le Havre, Dieppe and Boulogne. For over a week, trains left the city's Central station every hour, taking men often still bloody from the battlefield to military and civilian hospitals all over Britain. Rumours of the disaster travelled with them. Returning soldiers spared their loved ones the worst details. With others, they were often less delicate. When one train heading for Scotland pulled into a northwestern station en route, a soldier asked a group of women the name of the station. 'Accrington,' the women replied. 'Accrington?' the soldier shouted as the train pulled away: 'The Accrington Pals! They've been wiped out!'

As local anxieties grew nationwide, civic dignitaries petitioned the War Office for reports of their battalions. Women besieged town halls and the offices of regional newspapers begging for news. The lucky ones received urgent letters of reassurance from sons and husbands who had survived the battle. Those that didn't were condemned to wait, forced to assume the worst. Some had their assumptions precipitously confirmed by receiving their own letters back, the envelopes stamped simply 'KILLED'. But it would be weeks and months before the machinery of state was able to officially confer on its people – household by household – the true scale of the losses. The country was dumbstruck. Some postmen resigned.

The sense of national grief was amplified by the geographical concentration of the casualties. In one day the capital itself had suffered over 5,000 killed or wounded. The casualties for Manchester were 3,000; for Belfast, 1,800; Glasgow, Edinburgh, Newcastle, Bradford, Leeds and Birmingham, over 1,000 each; Durham, Liverpool, Sheffield, Lincoln, Derby, Nottingham, Wolverhampton and Cambridge each sustained losses of several hundred. By this stage of the war, the cost of modern battles was not unknown. In towns like Barnsley, Grimsby, Accrington and Salford, the curtains of terraced houses had been drawn before. But not in the whole street. Some town areas and villages had simply lost all their young men. Families had too. The two sons of one Belfast mother, a Mrs Mabin, had joined the 36th Division in 1914. Both were killed on 1 July. When the local Shankill post office noticed the two familiar buff-coloured envelopes, it held one of them back for two days.[6]

It was not just the numbers: it was who the numbers were. For centuries the British people had viewed their ordinary soldiers with suspicion, if not contempt – they were drunkards, chancers and vagabonds destined at best for an anonymous hole in the ground. But the soldiers whose names were now scrawled in their tens of thousands on government stationery were not such men. To the country that mourned them, they were a different breed entirely, one that had passed into legend before even putting on uniform: the valiant servants of Empire who in the hour of need had selflessly downed their tools and ledgers and together marched off to war. Within a matter of hours, this noble army seemed to have gone. Its wounded survivors, too numerous to hide from the public gaze, were limbless, sightless, senseless or missing half their face. The bereaved were presented with a Pre-Raphaelite image of their beloved's death: peaceful, immutable, intact under a cross of blinding white. But it was a vision they found hard to hold on to. From 1 July alone, there was not enough left of 7,000 soldiers even to know who they were.

In a single battle on a single day, Britain had lost more soldiers than in the first four months of the war: just short of the 21,000 who died in the three years of the Boer War and over four times the number of British servicemen and women who have lost their lives in the line of duty since the end of the Second World War. The first day of the Somme remains the costliest day in British military history.

The country's previous most bloody battle, at Waterloo, was over by nightfall. By the evening of 1 July 1916, the Battle of the Somme had only just begun. It continued into the quagmires of late autumn. When it came to an end, no gap had been torn in the German defences, no French town had been retaken, and the remnants of Britain's volunteer army had mostly dissolved in the mud. By 18 November 1916, one British soldier had been killed or wounded for every 2 cm of their army's six-mile advance. The four-and-a-half-month battle had cost over half the total number of British casualties, both military (from all three services) and civilian, in the whole of the Second World War.

Current historians are inclined to frame the Somme as an essential stepping-stone to winning the war, and even to conclude that the sacrifice of 1 July was 'justified' by the allies' eventual victory. Such assessments might have offered some consolation to the grieving yet still jingoistic millions of 1916. They would have meant less ten years later. In the decades that followed the Armistice, it appeared to a shattered nation that the only result of the Somme and its opening day (like the 'Great' war they came to symbolise) was death and untellable suffering on a scale it had never known; their only purpose, to be remembered. A hundred years later, the purpose seems the same.

The rural landscape of the 1 July battlefield now shows little trace of what happened there. The splintered stumps of trees are woods once again, as ancient as they looked before the fighting. The villages along the front, once pulverised to rubble, now stand as exact replicas of their former selves, their church spires reaching up from identical

---

6   While Mrs Mabin nearly had the misfortune to hear the news of the death of both her sons simultaneously, she was not the mother who suffered the greatest loss on 1 July. Mary Donaldson of Ballyloughlan in County Down had three sons in the 13th Royal Irish Rifles: John (aged 26), James (aged 23) and Samuel (aged 21). All three were killed on the south bank of the Ancre on 1 July. Another three brothers from the province, Privates Andrew, David and Robert Hobbs, attacking with the 9th Royal Irish Fusiliers on the opposite side of the river (from the position where Panorama ⑤ was taken), were also killed in the battle's first hour. (A fourth Hobbs brother, Herbert, was wounded in the attack on the Schwaben Redoubt but survived.) But perhaps the most tragic loss of all was suffered by a widow from Newfoundland, Mrs Lydia Ayre, who lost her two sons and her two nephews on 1 July. 'By their death,' reported a newspaper, 'Mrs Ayre has lost every member of her family.'

footprints. The fields, ploughed and sown every year since the battle, bear no scar of trenches or shell holes. Even the subtle bands of chalk that once betrayed the armies' front lines are now barely discernible, even from the air. The great 'harvest of iron', once piled by the tonne on every roadside, has dwindled to a handful of shells a season. The pickets and wire once used by farmers to supplement their fencing have now all but rusted away. Only the cemeteries remain as new as ever. Some still bear the names the soldiers gave them: Blighty Valley, Crucifix Corner, Owl Trench, Thistle Dump. All 63 in the area of the 1 July fighting stand as immaculate as when they were created, their lawned paths rolled and striped like a bowling green, their regiments of graves as white as when they were hewn, their inscriptions as crisp as when they were chiselled.

Today these 'silent cities' and the memorials and fields around them remain places of pilgrimage, no less solemn after the passing of a century. Every day, the arches of Lutyens's memorial are filled with silhouetted figures gazing up in awe at the endless names of the missing. The stories of Quigg, Cather and McFadzean are hourly intoned by old Irish soldiers on the lawns of the Ulster Memorial. Every summer, hundreds of schoolchildren are daily decanted from buses at Beaumont Hamel, Thiepval and the foot of the Montagne de Cappy, their voices instinctively dropped to a murmur. Tracksuited teenagers sidestep silently along the rows of graves. Small children are led by the hand to plant small wooden crosses on the graves of soldiers born over a century before them. In the 1920s, an average of 10,000 people a year travelled to the Somme to visit the graves of sons, fathers and husbands. In 2015, 300,000 made the same journey to visit the graves of men they had never known.

The last surviving soldiers of the trenches have been gone for nearly a decade. Even the grandsons of those who grieved are getting old. But while the Great War must slowly recede in our collective memory, it seems likely that the story of the middle day of its middle year never will.